Mahesh Dattani

Themes, Techniques and Issues

Edited by

Bishun Kumar

Neha Arora

Published by

ATLANTIC

PUBLISHERS & DISTRIBUTORS (P) LTD

7/22, Ansari Road, Darya Ganj, New Delhi-110002
Phones : +91-11-40775252, 40775214, 23273880, 23275880
Fax : +91-11-23285873
Web : www.atlanticbooks.com
E-mail : orders@atlanticbooks.com

Branch Office: Chennai
Phones : +91-44-48531784, 28291383
E-mail : chennai@atlanticbooks.com

Reprint 2019

Printed & bound in India by Atlantic Print Services

Dedicated to

Our Parents

and

Teachers

Preface

Mahesh Dattani can be acclaimed as a shining star in the world of Indian drama in English for his attempt to write his plays directly in a foreign tongue and twisting it to suit the Indian audience. Moreover, he has pioneered the re-evolution of Indian theatre and broken the hegemony of English drama in the world. He is an actor, director, script writer, dancer and social reformer, all fused in one. His plays are an experiment of a variety of themes, techniques and issues prevailing in Indian society and representation of concurrent cultural dynamism under the pressures of postmodern and postcolonial India.

What fascinated me to write on Dattani is his changing themes, issues and techniques play after play such as *Tara, Final Solutions, Morning Raga, Seven Steps around the Fire, Thirty Days in September, Do the Needful, The Big Fat City* and *Brief Candle*, his innovation and choice of subject matter. His theatrical journey begins from where other dramatists shuffle themselves. He has not only dared to portray incest, homosexuality, child sex, lesbian and gay boldly on the stage, but also compelled the society to relocate and redefine human sexuality. He, at the same time, attacks on the heinous acts like child sex and incest. Staging the taboo is a big challenge for a dramatist which Dattani not only accepts but also overcomes successfully.

The contemporary period has an ardent need for evolution and international recognition of Indian drama for both the purposes—as a mode of communication and as a projection of ethnic culture in the global market. Dattani has sufficed this very need of the country giving high stature to art, literature and culture of India.

The anthology *Mahesh Dattani: Themes, Techniques and Issues* is a modest attempt to observe his plays from various perspectives and to assess the contribution of his plays to the society. Thus, it is a new venture in the field of research and should prove profitable for the young researchers.

The book will be immensely beneficial for the students and teachers of Indian English literature, particularly Indian English drama.

Bishun Kumar
Neha Arora

Acknowledgements

This editorial pursuit *Mahesh Dattani: Themes, Techniques and Issues* is an upshot of a synthesized effect of motivation, inspiration, cooperation, suggestion, guidance and moral, physical and economic support of many persons. We are indebted to our teacher, guide and mentor Prof. S.Z.H. Abidi, former Head of the Department of English and Modern European Languages, University of Lucknow and currently Head Department of Languages and Dean Faculty of Humanities and Social Sciences, Integral University, Lucknow, for clarifying the theoretical concepts, developing critical thinking and orienting literary calibre in us. We extend our gratitude to our research guides, Dr. Nasrin, and Dr. V.P. Singh, Professors in the Department of English and Modern European Languages, University of Lucknow for their help and encouragement. We are also grateful to our teacher, Dr. R.P. Singh, Associate Professor in the Department of English and Modern European Languages, University of Lucknow for suggesting the topic for anthology and motivating us to edit it. We are also thankful to our friend, Dr. Ajay Chaubey, Assistant Professor in the Department of English, National Institute of Technology, Uttarakhand.

We shall always be indebted to our parents who remain the guiding star and propelling force behind us.

Finally, we thank the entire team of Atlantic Publishers & Distributors (P) Ltd., New Delhi for their cooperation and editorial support and all those who have helped us directly or indirectly and whom we could not mention here individually.

Bishun Kumar
Neha Arora

Contents

Introduction

In the world of Indian English theatre, Mahesh Dattani is a name for the fusion of an actor, director, author and a social thinker—all in one—that earns him the reputation of a "new avant-garde".[1] He knows what theatre is. For him, "it is a composite art, in which the author, the actor and the stage manager all combine to produce the total effect" (Worsfold, William Basil, *Judgment in Literature*, qtd. by B. Prasad in *A Background to the Study of English Literature,* 200: 73). Emerging as a "shining star"[2] in the world of Indian English drama, Dattani is undoubtedly indebted to the heritage of theatre in India, his predecessors and the classical Sanskrit theatre. The drama, both as a performing art and as a genre, has its roots in the classical Indian audience of 3rd century BC. The nation has had a great tradition to be proud of the poetics of the classical Sanskrit theatre that began with Bharata Muni's famous treatise *Natyashastra* which is considered as an additional *Veda*.

On the point of view of historiography of the theatrical art, evolution of Indian English drama requires looking back towards the origin of theatre in India. The aesthetics of performing art is not a new evolution to the Indian audience; rather it had been a prominent mode of amusement in classical India. Bharat Muni's *Natyashashtra* has already worked as "poetics of stage craft"[3] and initiated a "legislative paradigm for dramaturgy" for future generations and had claimed the significance of theatrical art in human life as, "Theatre is life. There is no art, no life, no craft, no learning, and no action which cannot be seen in it" (Ghosh, Manmohan. *Natyashashtra Ascribe to Bharat Muni* ed. and trans. 2007: 7).

However, Indian theatre in English is a late development of colonial India. Englishization of classical drama is a mark of colonial power that began with the imitation of English drama introduced by the British academicians with the double purpose—the first to acculturate Indians in British culture to demean indigenous culture of India, and the second to teach English language through English literature, the only medium available for teaching English language. Despite influences of modernism, postmodernism, postcolonialism and various theories of the drama in the world on Indian theatre, its soul rests within the parameter of *Natyashashtra*.

Impact of British colonization on the performing art and the decolonizing spirit of India—the passion for 'writing back', enhanced the ambit of Indian theatre not only within the national geographies but also across the boundaries. Indian drama required the power for fighting against the colonial dominance and also to compete with the international stage which was possible only through acquiring international language that is English. Thus, cumulative force, that is fascination towards English, anti-colonial drive, decolonizing intent and undoubtedly the zeal for international recognition on the world stage gave birth to Indian English Drama.

Indian English drama evolved much before Dattani's theatrical world, in the beginning of 19th century when the struggle for freedom was on its peak. It started its course of journey with 'the imitation' of language and style of British drama but its themes and subject matter were entirely of contemporary India—the India that was blazing with the fire of resistance against British governance. Krishna Mohan's *The Persecuted* (1837) is the first play in the history of Indian English drama that deals with the conflict between fading Hindu culture and prevailing Western ideas. However, it lacked proper form and technique. In the same series, Michael Madhusuadan Dutt's *Is This Called Civilization?* (1871) is an attack on the degradation of Indian culture in British regime and is known for the beginning of proper drama in English in India. In 19th century, for the lack of expertise in English language, playwrights in English were very few but this situation could not affect the eternal fame and growth of Indian drama. Towards the beginning of twentieth century, India produced a number of dramatists writing in English and in regional dialects as well. The aesthetics of performing art explored in the *Natyashashtra* was fused in the entire land of the country. Thus, the country gave birth to many "competing Shakespeares".[4]

The influence of postcolonialism, decolonization, postmodern conditions and desire for recognition on the international stage prepared the ground for translation of Sanskrit and Bhasha plays into English. From the phase of 'imitation' of British drama it acquired the phase of 'translation' of plays written in regional languages which we call Bhasha plays/theatre. However, the trend of cultural and linguistic translation into regional languages had already begun in pre-Independence India that flourished in post-Independence India. While translating the regional plays, the real flavor of India and its cultural ethos remained a unique attraction for the audience. To retain the taste of Indianness in Indian English drama even need for twisting the English tongue was inevitable. Mulk Raj Anand, a dramatist and novelist, once at the Drama Seminar organized by the Sangeet Natak Akadami held in April, 1956, had predicted that the new theatre would "have to speak the language of India if it [was] to become real, and even though the experimental theatre may go on playing in the English language, we [would] have to mould our spoken tongue to our purpose" (Proceedings, 344).

Thus, the trend of translation took the place of transcreation which was carried forward by the dramatists like Rabindranath Tagore (1861 – 1941; the recipient of Nobel Prize for *Gitanjali* in 1913), who contributed plays such as *Visarjan, Chandalika, The Post Office*, etc. For him it is said, "If you cry because the sun has gone out of your life, your tears will prevent you from seeing the stars". Tagore stated that his works sought to articulate "the play of feeling and not of action". Sri Aurobindo (15 August 1872 – 5 December 1950) has gifted us his plays like, *Perseus the Deliverer*, *Vasavadutta*, *Radoguna*, *The Viziers of Bassora* and *Eric*. Harindranath Chattopadhyay began his career with a brilliant comedy *Abu Hassan* (1918). Next to follow were A.S.P. Ayyar's *In the Clutch of the Devil* (1926) and *The Trial of Science for the Murder of Humanity* (1942). P.A. Krishnaswamy's fame rests on his verse play *The Flute of Krishna*. T.P. Kailasam is regarded as the "father of modern Kannada drama" with *The Burden* (1933), *Fulfillment* (1933), *The Purpose* (1944), *Karna* (1964) and *Keechaka* (1949) written in English. Women were also not far behind in contributing to the expansion of Indian English drama in the pre-Independence era. Bharati Sarabhai wrote two plays, *The Well of the People* (1943) and *Two Women* (1952). With J.M. Lobo Prabhu, the pre-Independence Indian English drama came to an end and 'New India', the free India was born. His prominent plays are *Mother of New India: A Play of Indian Village in Three Acts* (1944) and *Death Abdicates* (1945).

The 1960s, the decade when Dattani was opening his sensory eyes to watch and understand the world, claims the emergence of great names such as Nissim Ezekiel with his *Nalini* and *Sleep Walkers*, Gieve Patel with his *Princes* and *Savaksa*, and Pratap Sharma with his *A Touch of Brightness* and *The Professor has a War Cry*. The other famous names of this period are Gurucharan Das' *Larins Sahib*, Dina Mehta's *Brides Are Not for Burning (Lady Is Not for Burning)*, *Mythmakers* and Cyrus Mistry's *Doongaji House*. The genre kept propelling through centuries to come out of classical Sanskrit tradition to the present niche of multicultural theatre. Earlier it was restricted to the elite/classical Indian language Sanskrit, confined within a coterie section of the people. Over a period of time, dramatists began to explore other regional languages as well to bring Indian theatre out of coteries.

Thus, with the emergence of playwrights like Badal Sircar, Vijay Tendulkar, Girish Karnad, Habib Tanvir, Indira Parthasarathy, Asif Currimbhoy, Mahasweta Devi and Mahesh Dattani, the face of Indian English drama underwent a drastic change; for these contemporary dramatists started playing not only out of the coteries but also incorporated innovations in techniques and themes in drama with a complete breakaway with traditional drama form. It laid the foundation of a new era in Indian English drama which revisits history, recreates and re-incarnates myths and legends, reorganizes folklores to suit the contemporary socio-political issues and prepared the suitable ground for Dattani's theatrical world. And the plays of the following writers proved to be assets for Dattani.

Badal Sircar (15 July, 1925–13 May, 2011) took theatre to the streets and dismissed the derogatory notion that "street theatre is not an art". He founded his own theatre group, *Shatabdi* to bring acting out of proscenium theatre. Delineating the existentialist philosophy of life, he wrote *Evam Indrajit*, *Baki Itihas*, etc. which rocked not only the national but the international stage also. Safdar Hashmi was yet another practitioner of street theatre. The influence was soon to be seen on Tripurari Sharma. Her company, Alarippu, performed plays in the streets, dedicated them to the unheard voices and unarticulated political and social issues. His rise as a prominent playwright in 1960s is seen as the coming of the age of Modern Indian playwriting in Bengali, just as Vijay Tendulkar did it in Marathi, Mohan Rakesh in Hindi, and Girish Karnad in Kannada. However, Mahesh Dattani, instead of taking the already trodden road, explored the new path. Unlike Sircar, Dattani deals with social philosophy and has prepared a space for theatre in the hearts of the people even in the age of multimedia and 3-D industry.

Vijay Tendulkar (6 January 1928 – 19 May, 2008) has to his credit, 28 full-length plays, 7 collections of one-act plays, 6 collections of children's plays besides writing short stories, a novel and several film scripts. He is celebrated as the "playwright of the millennium", and his plays are accurate and sensitive portrayal of social issues that deal with the themes of alienation of the modern individuals, contemporary politics, man-woman relationships, etc. Some of his prominent plays are *Silence! The Court is in Session*, *Sakharam Binder* (1972), *Ghasiram Kotwal* (1972), *Kamala* (1981), *Kanyadaan* (1983), etc. His plays are about an enquiry into the pattern of growing violence in society and its relevance to contemporary theatre. But Tendulkar's *Ghāshirām Kotwāl* reflects the rise of Shiv Sena in Maharashtra in the 1970s. If Tendulkar's plays raise social issues of modern age, Dattani's plays raise the social issues of contemporary post-modern age.

Girish Karnad (19 May 1938) is an internationally acclaimed writer with many feathers in his cap. He is a poet, a playwright, actor, director, critic, translator, all rolled into one. His depth into Indian mythology and the dexterity with which he re-moulds the ancient stories as per the contemporary needs, is commendable.

Be it *Yayati* (1961), *Hayavadana* (1971), *Tughlaq* (1964), or *Naga Mandala*, his creativity is beyond excellence. *Hayavadana* was based on a theme drawn from *The Transposed Heads*, a novella (1940) by Thomas Mann which is originally found in the 11th century Sanskrit text *Kathasaritsagara*. Herein, he employed the folk theatre form of *Yakshagana*. Unlike Karnad, Dattani's plays are a critique of degrading humanity in the age of overgrowing corporate culture, dominance of technology and metropolitanism.

Habib Tanvir, the playwright, theatre director, poet, actor and founder of Naya Theatre, a theatre company in Bhopal (1959), is primarily known for his famous works like *Agra Bazar*, *Charandas Chor*, *Shatranj ke Mohrey*, *Jis Lahore Nai Dekhya*, *Zahreeli Hawa*, to name a few. He joined the Progressive Writers' Association as an actor and was an integral part of the Indian People's Theatre Association (IPTA). If Tanvir's aspect is social, Dattani's is biological and psychological.

Asif Currimbhoy is believed to have actually founded the modern Indian drama where Dattani is flourishing. His dramas like *The Doldrummers*, *The Dumb Dancer*, *Goa*, etc. ooze out the sensuality of the modern age. His characters are social outcastes caught in the whirlpool of social and political system, while Dattani focuses on the centrification of the decentred whom we call "third gender".

What is remarkable is that these playwrights wrote mostly in the regional languages. Their plays were translated either by themselves or by someone else and some of them have been transcreated for the purpose of acclaiming their significance at the world stage. But Mahesh Dattani has jumped up to write directly into English leaving his precursors far behind, though, not in the English of the elite and sophisticated class, but in the English of the educated urban middle-class Indians, to make his plays completely Indian. And his experiment with the foreign language is embraced wholeheartedly by the theatre lovers, whether in India or England or America. He preferred to write in English, despite hailing from Gujarat and Bangalore so that he could connect to his people. Responding to whether he perceives writing in English as a hurdle, Dattani avers:

> English has a ubiquitous presence throughout the country. I was born and brought up in Bangalore and therefore have an urban sensibility. I performed my first play there. My plays are about what I see, feel and understand. Since I write in English, I guess my plays would appeal immediately to the people who have grown up with the language; yet what the plays present is an Indian lifestyle and so would be significant for all Indians. (An Interview with Tutun Mukherjee, "I Do Not Write Merely to Be Read")

Dattani, the young Indian playwright, the winner of prestigious Sahitya Akadami Award for Dramaturgy, was born on 7th of August 1958 at Porbandar in Gujarat, educated at Baldwin High School and St. Joseph College of Arts and Science and received postgraduate degree in Marketing and Advertising Management. His zeal for acting was perplexedly awakened by his father's talks about his days in Bombay when he visited theatres at Bhangwadi to see Gujarati Musical Drama. His father "would talk about legends like, Motibai, Miss Shyamabai, and comedian Chagan 'Romeo'" (*Me and My Plays*, 2014: 4). His "virgin sense of dramaturgy"[5] started turning to maturity when he saw real people on the stage, unlike in the movies, "I was stuck by the loud voices of the actors and their loud costumes" (*Me and My Plays*, 2014: 6) while watching Madhu Rye's acclaimed Gujarati play *Koi Pan Ek Phool Nu Naam Bolo To* (Say the Name of a Flower). He was nervous for he could not get an opportunity to act in a play but he maintained his natural instinct of acting through listening attentively to the stories of his father, "I recall becoming more attentive to my father's stories of Bhangwadi in the past and the theatres he used to frequent during his business trip to Bombay" (*Me and My Plays,* 2014: 8).

A shy schoolboy, Mahesh who began acting with the role of an angel, shivering and trembling on the stage in an annual school production, usually a Christmas pageant, has today achieved the stature of an acclaimed world dramatist, script-writer, dancer, actor and director. Dattani was born of the theatre and for the theatre. The credit to bring his innate talent out of closet goes to his schoolmate Ramesh for he played along as a source of great amusement to his parents and cousins, as Dattani himself admits:

> The actor in me did come out of closet on some occasions. I remember a schoolmate Ramesh, who was as timid as me. I was not sure how interested he was in drama but he played along, since it was a source of great amusement to his parents and cousins. I would take a fairy tale like 'Snow White' and get everyone on Ramesh's Terrace. We would rehearse the scenes and choreograph a little dance. (*Me and My Plays,* 2014: 9-10)

Unfortunately, it did not last very long since Ramesh grew bored with the whole thing. It turned out that his interest was in cricket. For this Dattani still hates cricket; he slips to say, "May be I still hate the game: It robbed me of a potential collaborator" (*Me and My Plays,* 2014: 11). The next significant thing to enhance the taste of drama in him was Alan Ayckbourn's *Table Manners,* an English comedy of manners performed by the Bangalore Little Theatre or (BLT). This was the first English play which he watched on a public stage with his friend's friend that very soon turned him a champion of Indian English drama. At the same time the Bangalore Little Theatre or (BLT) was looking for volunteers for their future production. Dattani fills a membership form and officially gets a membership. This proves a great achievement for Dattani at the age of eighteen for he started getting BLT newsletters.

The zeal for acting was in his mind and heart. He would read newsletters every word and hope there was a casting call. Once there was! He showed up but he was rejected, rejected once, twice, thrice,...many times for some years because his physical structure was against the acting profession. He knew, "There were two things going against me, my thin, nasally voice and my effeminate gestures" (*Me and My Plays,* 2014: 11). This shows that the theatres, especially directors in the boyish days of Dattani were in the grip of colonial parameter of cast selection even in the post-Independence period. The term "effeminate"[6] is culturally a self-realized drawback which is an impact of the colonial acculturation and is a colonial blot of 'othering' and degradation on his personality. The occident stereotypes the orient as, "He was now religious but superstitious, clever but devious, chaotically violent but effeminately cowardly" (Sardar, Ziauddin and Borin Van Loon. *Introducing Cultural Studies: A Graphic Guide,* 2010: 86). His formation of his own theatre organization, "Playpen" in 1984 and his success to achieve the position at world stage, is an answer to all colonial bugs.

Moreover, he was brought up in a soil that has its roots deeply penetrated in the classical Indian theatre that went on changing its face, form and technique to struggle for its position in everyday contemporary changing situations, to adapt to the psyche of post-industrial man and at the same time to compete with the theatres of the world which can today proudly be called Indian English drama.

Dattani is a fusion of Kalidas—a unique metaphor of love, and Shakespeare—an incomparable playwright of the populace. He is the dramatist of all the people of the rich, the marginalized, the ignored, the corporate, the metropolitans and the poor, but especially of the marginals, the betrayed, the dispossessed, the degraded, and of the ignored people. He can justifiably be called "man of people".[7] For choosing characters from the ignored humanity, today he is recognized among the world's most popular playwrights. Moreover, the playwright has already admitted, "I write for my milieu, for my time and place, middle class and urban Indians...my dramatic tension arise from people who aspire to freedom from society.... (*The Hindu*: Out of the Closet, On the Screen. March 09, 2003).

Moreover, the themes and techniques employed and the issues raised in his plays are fusion of ideas of the novelists like Dickens—the writer of hungry forties, Mulk Raj Anand—a humanist and social critic, and playwrights like G.B. Shaw—who deals with social problems, Henrik Ibsen—who raised burning social issues, all of which embraced people facing miserable condition.

His plays are a result of his collective experiences. His definition of theatre is that of participatory and he writes in a way that his readers/audience would need to make efforts to understand the incidents on the stage. He would not serve them on silver plates.

However, it should not be concluded that Dattani comes as a teacher to his audience. He does not advocate any change as such or conveys any message; what he does is simply hold a mirror to the society. In an interview with Anita Nair he confesses that "theatre to me is a reflection of what you observe. To do anything more would be to become didactic and then it ceases to be theatre" ("Mahesh Dattani—The Invisible Observer").

He perceives drama as a potent medium to communicate his thoughts/observation across, awaking the audiences from their deep slumber. The audiences are never spared any respite; they are compelled to develop a critical insight. In his interview by Roy, Dattani states:

> The function of drama, in my opinion, is not merely to reflect the malfunction of society but to act like freak mirrors in a carnival and to project grotesque images of all that passes for normal in our world. It is ugly. It is funny. (Roy, *The Hindu*, 15 March 2002)

"Powerful and disturbing", this is how D.J.R. Bruckner praises Mahesh Dattani in the *New York Times* and the words directly comment on the carefully chosen themes of the playwright. Dattani sets himself apart from his contemporaries by plunging into the lives of middle-class Indians and bringing them/their issues on the stage. His plays are serious and thought-provoking; whether it is the reader or the spectator, he/she cannot keep himself/herself aloof from the events he/she is witnessing. Just as Brecht creates a wall between the audience and the actors/stage, Dattani too believes that contemporary drama should not suspend the rational faculty of the audience. His formula is to estrange the spectators/readers from the stage/text and allow them to think.

The techniques such as the play-within-the-play, direct speech, aside addressed to the audiences, music, dance, etc. can be easily observed as thoroughly exploited by him. Dattani makes maximum and intelligent use of space and environment; he is adept at presenting simultaneous action, slow motion, choreography, etc. Following Brecht, he too uses minimal characters.

Conforming to the trend of the twentieth century, Dattani too is cautious of the form and content of his dramas. One of the striking features of his plays is the stage direction. His plays are not meant to be read within the closed walls; rather to be staged for the audience, hence much focus is on the techniques employed. As in Shaw, in Dattani too we get elaborate stage directions. With his experiments and innovations he has enriched the Indian English drama. The Italian director John McRae remarks in a note on the play:

> Mahesh Dattani is always adventurous in his way of using the theatrical space at his disposal: multiple levels, breaking the bounds of Proscenium, wondrously inventive use of lighting to give height, breadth and depth. (*On a Muggy Night in Mumbai* in *Collected Plays: Mahesh Dattani*, 2000: 45)

Dattani seems to enjoy playing with the innovations in dialogue delivery too. Unlike the traditional dramatists, he does not use 'aside' to bring out the thoughts of his characters, and instead introduces the technique of 'thought'. It is followed by 'voice-over'. He even makes the dead characters interact with the living ones. He prefers to resort to the flashback technique to bring back the past to reinforce the present. The action period in his plays is very short. In writing about the stark, naked and ugly reality, he does not attempt to idealize the world. He exudes confidence even on controversial subjects like incest, child abuse, etc. His plays are mere 'presentations', leaving the audiences thinking. To quote Bijay Kumar Das:

> Dattani's plays are 'lokdharmi' as opposed to 'natyadharmi' of Sanskrit plays. If 'natyadharmi' plays conform to the conventions of the theatre, 'lokdharmi' caters to the way of the world. In his plays Dattani depicts the characters in contemporary life who reveal themselves before the audience in realistic terms. (*Form and Meaning in Mahesh Dattani's Plays*, 2008: 167)

The endings of his plays always leave the audiences thinking and soul searching. He does not provide them with any cooked up conclusions. It is not that his characters are trapped in the complicated situations; he impels them to have a deeper insight to realize that it is actually "we all" who are caught in the whirlpool of our complexities. He mirrors our own image.

As aforesaid, Dattani chooses the problems of common masses and brings them to limelight; he, thus, is the Indian Dickens/Shaw/Ibsen/Brecht. His dramas are the nativized form of "Drama of Ideas" exposing the 'condition of India/ns' using the Brechtian Epic Theatre.

His plays discuss the sensitive issues, exploring the gamut of relationships, and the matrix of entangled issues form the core of his plays. To quote his views:

> Thematically, I talk about the areas which the individual feels exhausted. My plays are about people who are striving to expand 'this' space. They live on the fringe of the society and are not looking for acceptance, but are struggling to grab as much fringe-space for themselves as they can. (*Collected Plays*, 2000: xiii)

Conforming to his taste and following his inclination, Mahesh Dattani proceeds to explore and expose the subjects that need proper address, the subjects that live with us, the subjects we breathe life into, yet we are not courageous enough to face them. Our middle-class morality restrains us and brushes them under the carpet. However, Dattani's plays come as vacuum cleaners, incessantly cleaning the dirt of the society. Issues like incest, homosexuality, eunuchs, female infanticide, gender issues, etc. are not new for any of us (the reader/the audience or the writers). The difference lies in the treatment. The ubiquitous yet sensitive issues need to be dealt with utter care lest they should cause a spark in the otherwise dormant society. Without being didactic, Dattani manages to sensitize his people of the gravity of the subject.

His characters are you and me; his subjects are 'our' stories. Yet the skill of converting the mundane into exciting is the hallmark of Dattani. He experiments with the unusual, yet close to us. Diving deep into the psyche of his characters, he projects the real men and women on the stage. His conviction sets him apart. Undeterred with the response of traditional audience, he treads ahead on the road of exposing various 'ignored' facets of society—the aspects we are generally ashamed to acknowledge. He has courage enough to call "a spade, a spade". Without romanticising with the issue, he frankly and boldly serves the reality to his audience, whether it is palatable to our taste buds or not. Be it discussing the case of *hijras* (eunuchs) or HIV/AIDS patients or the homosexuals or any other subaltern, he lays bare the hypocrite Indian society. To use N. Velmani's words:

> Dattani's plays expose the violence of our private thoughts and the hypocrisy of our public morals. They expose the dark secrets of the human consciousness that torment in the present. They reveal the physical and spatial awareness of Indian theatre on the one hand and the textual rigour of Ibsen and Tennessee Williams on the other hand. (*Drama in Indian Writing in English—Tradition and Modernity*: 16)

On being asked as to why does Dattani write such "heavy plays", he responded with a question, "Why do we lead such heavy lives?" For him, theatre helps in tearing down the mask and brings the reality directly in our face. In an interview with Erin B. Mee at the Bookery in Bangalore (August 27, 1996), Dattani favours writing about what one knows the best:

> I think one has to be true to one's own environment. Even if I attempted writing a play about the angst of rural Indian society, it wouldn't ring true, it would be an outsider's view—I could only hope to evoke sympathy, but never really to be a part of that unless I spend a lot of time there. I think there are enough issues and challenges in urban Indian society (the milieu I am a part of) and these automatically form the content of my work. (*Mahesh Dattani: Invisible Issues*, 19)

In the garb of comedy, Dattani serves the gravest issues on our platter—those happening around us, everyday, to whom we always tend to close our eyes, the same unpalatable issues we relish and take inside us when the chef is Dattani. For him, all issues are to be/should be in the mainstream and should be discussed openly—be it that of eunuchs, homosexuals, HIV/AIDS patients, etc.—as they all are very much a part of our society. His daring attempts have received varied responses from the audiences which is a blend of liberal and conservative mindsets. He projects the "complicated dynamics of the modern urban family" (Erin B. Mee, *Contemporary Indian Theatre: Three Voices*: 4).

To comment upon Dattani's language, it is lucid and easily understandable by the audiences who are as educated as are his characters; hence his language sounds convincing. Common masses find his plays capturing the sensibility and temperament of the urban elite. Domestic space/life of urban section of the society is primarily the locus of all his plays. His is the real India, the real people. Even his language is English spoken by the urban people (in its hybridised form). There is abundant use of code-mixing and code-switching. He finds a rapport with his audiences by using their issues and presenting them in their language. His plays are not meant to cater to the foreign audiences; they are for the urban Indians of twentieth century who frequently mix English with their native tongue (Hindi, Gujarati, Marathi, etc.). Since these people have removed the veil of conventional modesty, his characters too unabashedly talk about sex and other taboo subjects. They are real people who speak the real language of the contemporary urban Indian middle class and leave a lasting impact—their words echo in the ears of the audience. In brief, Dattani's plays feel and reproduce the unrest of the present age—the clash between tradition and modernity. In the Preface to *Collected Plays*, he writes:

> I am certain that my plays are a true reflection of my time, place and socio-economic background. I am hugely excited and curious to know what the future holds for me and my art in the new millennium in a country that has a myriad challenges to face politically, socially, artistically and culturally. (2000: xv)

The research papers included in this anthology explore and experiment with a variety of themes, techniques and issues dealt in the plays of Mahesh Dattani. The researchers give fresh insight for the close examination of Dattani's plays on various aspects.

Neha Arora in her paper entitled "*Brief Candle*: Life in Death or Death in Life?" deals with 'philosophy of optimism in life'.

The play is a dark comedy about the patients of 'Cancer disease' an approaching death face to face but Vikas, one of the patients, makes a plan to raise fund for the patients of such diseases. Dattani has made a beautiful attempt to pin point the value of 'hope' what we call "optimism" in life through Vikas's plan to stage a play costing the patients in the hospital such as Shanti, Amarinder and Vikas himself. Though the play deals with the real stories of the lives of the patients which are very pathetic, the author spots Dattani`s optimistic vision in handling the tragic traits in a comic way just as Charles Lamb in his essays narrates painful events of his life humourously. She locates Dattani's *Brief Candle* with Shakespeare's tragedy *Macbeth*, Tennyson`s "Ulysses" and Browning's "Rabbi Ben Ezra". The author has found the fusion of Albert Camus' Myth of Sisyphus and Sartre's philosophy of existentialism. The disease 'Cancer' in the play is a loaded term, for it reflects not only a lethal disease but the cancer of society that means all evils prevailing in the society eating up the good within man and have become an untreatable disease. Still the man with a divine instinct makes every effort to make the society 'heaven' till the last moment.

The next paper by Bishun Kumar "Postmodernism in Dattani's *Where There is a Will*" explores the major technique employed in the play and the impression it leaves on the contemporary world of theatre. Dattani, being a product of post-colonialism and postmodernism cannot ignore its impact on himself. Kumar in his paper observes how Dattani has blurred the traditional techniques, like aside, supernatural machinery, etc. and has fused past with present. In the paper, Hasmukh's "will" has been recognized as the parody of neocolonialism exercised on his own family members. Hasmukh, an orthodox businessman, is always in conflict with his son Ajit, daughter-in-law, Preeti and his wife Sonal for he does not find them to be able to carry on the heritage of family business. Instead, he invests his faith on his "keep" Kiran who, he thinks, would teach the lesson to his family members and keep uplifting his company too, but finds himself trapped in his own design.

Though problematizing gender studies is a postmodern offshoot, yet its roots are spread deeply in the society from the very beginning of civilization on the earth to the present-day metropolitan culture. In her paper "Mahesh Dattani's *Seven Steps around the Fire:* Travails of the Third Sex" Sarika Kanjlia raises burning issues of the identity crisis, degradation and social outcasting of the third sex, namely gays, hijras (eunuchs). The author has successfully unfurled the veil under which hijras' lives are suppressed. Her critical approach to the story of the murder of a eunuch, Kamala portrayed in the play finds that despite having a history of 4000 years and having done many significant roles in the society, their plight has never been recognized. Their condition is many more times miserable than that of women who are at least, considered to be human beings. Dattani, she claims, is perhaps the first person to have brought these eunuchs on the centre from the margins. It is Uma, wife of Suresh, the jail superintendent and the daughter of Vice Chancellor of Bangalore University, who resolves to take research project in sociology and determines to resolve the mystery of Kamala's murder. In her paper she underlines that men are fascinated towards the beauty of these eunuchs and love to satisfy their orgasm, but once their lust is quenched they are treated as the wastes, the leavings, rather a lifeless thing and thrown into a bottomless abyss.

Dattani's eyes keep a vigil on the entire social behavior. He cross-examines through his X-ray capacity to bring out all that is lying under the several layers on the surface reality of the society. The bright looking outward features of social and familial relations are emotionally blackmailed and sexually harassed by the men with the dark desires. Mamta Khosla in her paper "Incest: Cause of Pain and the Rift between Mother and Daughter" deals with the problem of incest deep rooted in society. She examines Dattani`s play, *Thirty Days in September* which boldly brings false pride of the men, the hierarchy and their heinous act on the stage to lay bare what goes behind the patriarchal ostracism. The paper, through the characters like Mala Khatri and her mother Shanti, throws light on the child sexual abuse and incest, physical and emotional exploitation of both the females by their own close relative Vinay, the brother of Shanti. The paper underlines how Mala is exploited before the stage of puberty and turned into a whore knowing nothing about her life, identity and future except the sex. She could not get help even from her mother Shanti in the name of social prestige what she called the family decorum. The focus of the paper is on Shanti's mums that tell how women eternalize the plight for being helpless. Shanti could not protect her daughter for she herself had been sexually exploited by her own real brother Vinay at her tender age of eleven and was turned into a sex object to be always ready for his brother to serve her flesh ungrudgingly. The paper examines why women fail to lay bare the truths buried under the name of family decorum.

Bhaskar Lama in his paper entitled "Identity through the Trajectory of Trust and Distrust: Viewing Muslim Minority in the Modern Secular Framework through *Final Solutions*" has traced the burning issues in India having no final solution. Lama finds that the question of "identity" is an outcome of performative act of trust and distrust, inclusion and exclusion, us and them. Lama finds that religious strife between Hindus and Muslims is orchestrated, like a 'mirror' to scour for a platform where they could negotiate and understand each other's position. The paper highlights that the religious controversies and stereotyping has replaced the very future of secularism and modernism in post-partition India and focuses Dattani's purpose of evidencing the fact that, "Unless we shake off our prejudices in our psyche in our genes, we will always be found locked in combat... Arab against Jews, Whites against Blacks, Hindus against Muslims, and get no final solutions".

Dattani, even in the age of mechanism and commercialism, thinks upon the social issues that disrupt man's position and dislocate his existence constantly from what he stabilizes. Soumyadip Ghosh's article "Interrogating Social Conscience: Re-reading Dattani's *Where Did I Leave My Purdah?, The Big Fat City* and Karnad's *Wedding Album*" strikes at the basic hiatus between what the man craves for and what he really becomes, which results in his identity crisis, but the dramatist does not leave his audiences on the pathless island; rather he gives an indication that the crisis could be resolved by the victims themselves by dint of their urge to fight against the odds of the society and machinery. The paper also talks of the liaison of Indian theatre to tradition and modernity which creates the ambiguity by way of the entailment of multiplicity, variety and cultural heterogeneity within it. The author pinpoints Dattani's will to highlight socially hidden issues that might have been existing in Indian psyche but unfortunately they have never been given any importance so that they could attain both 'Page' and 'Stage.'

Yet another paper entitled, "Gendered Self: Postmodernist Handling of a Sensitive Issue in Mahesh Dattani's *Tara*" by Samina Parvin and Munira T. explores the elements of postmodernity in the play *Tara*. The authors highlight the playwright's art of merging facts with fiction even regarding a very sensitive issue. *Tara* is a play about the Siamese twins born conjoined from the chest down in which Dattani takes the liberty of making them boy and girl twins. The emotional separation of Tara and Chandan is replaced by mechanical (medical) separation. Since the play gives no clue, it offers a number of valid interpretations. Audiences and critics find it the play about feminism, gender discrimination, patriarchal dominance, fascination of middle-class women to have a male child, but the dramatist wishes to portray the complex nature of human sexuality. The paper interprets twins as the two selves of a human being—the male and the female—and the death of Tara during operation is a mark of suppression of man's own female self. Even the concept of taking Siamese conjoined twins is a rarest of the rare phenomenon and is a proof of postmodern thought of the playwright.

Despite many praises of being known for first Indian dramatist writing directly in English, Dattani could not be rewarded for writing in 'pure' or 'official' or in British English. Rituparna Das' paper "Trapped in Labyrinth: An Interplay of the Language Protest through Slang and Jargon in Mahesh Dattani's *Bravely Fought the Queen* and *On a Muggy Night in Mumbai*" examines the language used by the dramatist. The paper marks the 'slang', 'hybrid English', 'Indianized English' and Hindi terms, and searches for the reason of opting such terms while writing in English. The author reaches the conclusion that Dattani is bound to use mix language such as slang, code-switching and code-mixing to make his plays suitable for Indian urban middle class audience. He does not write for the working class.

Thus, she finds Dattani trapped between English and Hindi slang or colloquial language for the setting, the locale and the situations that are purely middle class urban Indian.

Cultural heritage of India flows in Dattani's blood, with performing art, instrumental play and art of music—all fused together to give shape to a playwright like Dattani. Besides, being an actor and director, he trained himself in western ballet under Molly Andre at Alliance Francaise to Bangalore (1984-87) and learnt *Bharatnatyam* under Chandrabhanga Devi and Krishna Rao at Bangalore (1986-90). Tuhin Majumdar and Nandini Maity's paper "Mahesh Dattani's Plays on Music and Dance: A Reading of *Morning Raga* and *Dance Like a Man*" explores playwright's unconditional love for dance and music. They find both the plays a projection of the dramatist's own self. *Morning Raga* is a play about carnatic music performed by casting like Shabana Azmi and Perizad Zorabian. The central figures Vashnavi, Swarnlatha and Pinkie are a creation of his own self.

The play *Dance Like a Man* deals with the theme of cultural significance of Bharatnatyam which was taken as derogatively, a feature of *nautch* girls only. The paper focuses on how Dattani has succeeded in defining the worth of music and dance in human life, throwing light on Jairaj and his wife Ratna taking the training of Bharatnatyam against the will of their parents. Moreover, it concludes with the impression that both these plays are about the meeting ground of the two worlds—the modern and the traditional and unite the past with the present.

Social norms and biological needs, though, are complementary to each other, yet social and legal conditions are man-made—a social construct that many times fails to define varying natural instincts and biological differences. Ayesha Anwar Warsi's paper "Rethinking Gender: A Critical Study of Dattani's *Do the Needful*" deals with a burning issue of homosexuality, a widening gulf between social norms and biological needs. Social norms make every effort to universalize and bring all human affairs in a state of equilibrium. It is this conflict in which Alpesh and Lata, the leading characters of the play, are crushed. The paper pinpoints the plight of homosexuals and lesbians in a conservative heterosexual society through Alpesh, a homosexual and Lata who loves sex fantasies and invites a debate on, "do the needful" as against "do the lawful".

No matter whether socially acceptable or not, any sexuality, whether traditional heterosexuality or queer homoeroticity, if it is a relationship based on consent, it is not a crime. But if it is forced, black-mailing, perverted and conditioning to quench one's sexual fantasies, it is an unpardonable crime. Moreover, if anyone forces the immature children, it is a heinous crime. Child sexual abuse has become a common problem of this postmodern society. Mustabshira Siddqui's paper "Lifting the Veil the Woman Speaks: A Critical Appraisal of Dattani's *Thirty Days in September*" draws our attention toward this burning issue of child sexual abuse and makes an attempt to highlight the playwright's greatest concern with the evils of society through Mala, a child character, a victim of sexual abuse in Dattani's play. At her tender age, she bears the wounds of the exploitation of her sex organs by her own maternal uncle Vinay, more than four times older than her. When she shouts with pain, she is blackmailed by a lure of chocolate offered by her uncle or by her own mother on the name of lord Krishna, an emblem of love and romance, or by the edibles of her choice.

Whether society recognizes it or not, sexualities other than hetero are as old as human civilization. The traces of alternative sexualities are there in epics, myths, legends and in ancient history. The people with alternative sexualities have got no identity of their own; they are rather, degraded and dislocated. Preeti Singh's paper "Relocating the Margins: A Study of Alternative Sexuality in Dattani's Plays" is an attempt at tracing Dattani's effort to relocate the recognition of gays, lesbians, etc. in the mainstream to have their own identity. The paper is a critique of conservative society and continuity of the civilization through the promotion of the heterosexuality and suppression of queer behavior. It marks how queer behavior is deemed to be an act of trespassing or ethical perversion, sometimes regarded as an abnormal behavior. It deals with the multiple perceptions of homosexuality such as taboo, alternate sexuality, minor sin, romanticity, antisocial, antinorms, unconventional and sometimes a heinous crime that deserves death penalty.

In academic parlance, gays and lesbians articulate boldly the plight and degradation of their race in the society. They even legally have been provided equal rights, but socially they face too many problems. Shoaib Ekram's paper entitled "Problems of Accepting the 'Other' in *On a Muggy Night in Mumbai*" explores the difficulties faced by the gays, homosexuals and lesbians in a conservative society and underlines the invisible wounds made in the personality of the people with alternative sexualities. Even those who, in theory, support their demands, in practice, make no place for accepting the 'other' as equal to them.

The contemporary period is an age of information and technology, more critically in the grip of over-professionalism, in practice of cut-throat policies and ambition of becoming rich, amassing affluence and enjoying the luxury life. In brief, the postmodern concept of "maximum riches and luxury life in least effort" has overshadowed the value of life, emotion, love, affection and relationship and we proudly call it metropolitan lifestyle. Ashish Kumar Sharma's paper entitled "Dattani's *The Big Fat City:* A Modern Waste Land" is a study of life in metropolitan cities in the light of the play *Big Fat City.* The author, taking privilege of reader response theory, validates his interpretation of what has been projected in the play. The city of Mumbai in which play has been set stands as an "unreal city", "a modern waste land" like that of Eliot's "The Waste Land" which was blazing with the fire of lust and mechanical relationship, while Dattan's Mumbai, "a modern waste land" is blazing with the fire of lust plus ambition of amassing money, and thus, promotes professional relationship. Thus, the paper brackets the metropolitan life—more a degradation and Mumbai—a representative of metropolitan cities in the world.

Bishun Kumar
Neha Arora

Notes

1. Dattani is the first person in India to write plays purely in English and have earned a worldwide reputation.

2. His (Dattani's) precursors attempted writing in English and gained recognition either through translation or through transcreation of their plays. Therefore, they may be called 'morning star' of Indian drama in English.
3. *Natyashashtra* is the first draft in India to have formulated the form, content and objectives of theatre.
4. The dramatists evolving from different states have widely been compared to William Shakespeare and have been termed as "the Shakespeare of West Bengal, of Kannad, and of Madhya Pradesh, etc."
5. Dattani himself admits in his book *Me and My Plays*, 2014: 6.
6. The term has been used derogatively for Dr. Aziz, a representative of the Orient by E.M. Forster in his novel *A Passage to India*.
7. Dattani has concerns for the problems of every man—common people and his plays deal with the issues of every man.

Works Cited

Aronson, Arnold. "Postmodern Design". *Theatre Journal* 43. The John Hopkins University Press. 1991. http://www.columbia.edu/~apa4/pdfs/Aronson_pomodesign.pdf. 9 Sep, 2012. Web.

Barry, Peter. *Beginning Theory: An Introduction to Literary and Cultural Theories*. Manchester and New York: Manchester University Press, 2002. Print.

Boulton, Marjorie. *The Anatomy of Drama*, New Delhi: Kalyani Publisher, 1985: 3. Print.

Das, Bijay Kumar. *Form and Meaning in Mahesh Dattani's Plays*. New Delhi: Atlantic Publishers & Distributors (P) Ltd., 2008. Print.

Dattani, Mahesh. *Collected Plays*. New Delhi: Penguin Books India Pvt. Ltd., 1994. Print.

Dattani, Mahesh. *Me and My Plays*. New Delhi: Penguin Books India Pvt. Ltd., 2014. Print.

Ghosh, Manomohan edited and trans. *Natyashashtra Ascribe to Bharat-Muni: A Treatise on Ancient Indian Dramaturgy and Histrionics*. Volume I & II, Varanasi: Chowkhambha Sanskrit Series Office, Reprint, 2007. Print.

Hutcheon, Linda. *A Poetics of Postmodernism: History, Theory, Fiction*. London and New York: Routledge, 1988. Print.

Karnad, Girish. *Author's Introduction to Three Plays*. Delhi: Oxford University Press, 1994: 3. Print.

——. *Three Plays: Naga Mandala, Hayavadana, Tughlaq*. Delhi: Oxford University Press, 1999. Print.

Multani, Angelie. *Mahesh Dattani: Critical Perspectives*. Ed. New Delhi: Pencraft International, 2011. Print.

Sardar, Ziauddin and Borin Van Loon. *Introducing Cultural Studies: A Graphic Guide*. Malta: Guttenberg Press, 2010: 86. Print.

Sircar, Badal. *Voyage in the Theatre*. Shri Ram Memorial Lectures Calcutta: 1992. s3.

——. *The Third Theatre*. Calcutta: Badal Sircar, 1978. 4. Print.

Velmani, N. "Drama in Indian Writing in English—Tradition and Modernity." *Language in India*, Vol. 13, No. 6: 16. Print.

Worsfold, William Basil. *Judgment in Literature*, qutd. by B. Prasad in *A Background to the Study of English Literature*. New Delhi: MacMillan Publishers, 2000: 73.

Contributors

Ashish Kumar Sharma is Assistant Professor in the Department of English in Babu Banarasi Das National Institute of Technology and Management, Lucknow and a research scholar in the University of Lucknow, Lucknow. He is working on Rana Bose, an Indian Diaspora in Canada. His areas of interest are Canadian Literature, Indian Theatre and Diaspora Literature.

Ayesha Anwar Warsi is Assistant Professor in the Department of English at Karamat Husain Muslim Girls' Postgraduate College, University of Lucknow, Lucknow. She has published many research papers in reputed National and International Journals.

Bhaskar Lama is research scholar in The English and Foreign Languages University, Hyderabad. He has published many papers in National and International Journals.

Bishun Kumar shares his knowledge as Assistant Professor in the Department of English in Babu Banarasi Das University, Lucknow (Uttar Pradesh) India and has achieved a Doctoral Degree on Mulk Raj Anand, a major author of the down trodden. He has edited four other volumes on varied areas which are *Major Voices in New Literatures in English*, *Transnational Passages: An Anthology of Diaspora Criticism*, *Discursive Passages: An Anthology of Diaspora Criticism*, and *Salman Rushdie: An Anthology of 21st Century Criticism*. Presently he is working on Cultural Studies in India and Corporate Culture.

Mamta Khosla is Assistant Professor in the Department of English at D.A.V. Centenary College, Faridabad, Haryana. She has many papers to his credit in National and International Journals.

Munira T. is Assistant Professor in the Department of English at Women's College, Aligarh Muslim University, Aligarh, Uttar Pradesh.

Mustabshira Siddiqui is Assistant Professor in the Department of English at Lucknow Christian Degree College, University of Lucknow, Lucknow and a research scholar in the same university. Her areas of interest are SAARC Literature, Postcolonial Theory, Gender Studies, African and Caribbean Literature.

Nandini Maity is Assistant Professor in the Department of English Language and Technical Communication in Saroj Mohan Institute of Technology, Hooghly, West Bengal. Having cleared UGC-NET, she is pursuing Ph. D in Comics from The University of Burdwan, West Bengal. She has published many papers in prestigious National and International Journals.

Neha Arora is Assistant Professor of English in the Department of English in Central University of Rajasthan, Ajmer, Rajasthan. She has achieved her doctoral degree on "From Margin to Mainstream: A Selected Study of Literature on Dalits" and her areas of specialization are Dalit Literature, Comparative Literature, African Literature, Indian Literature in English & in Translation, Bhasha Literatures and Postcolonial Studies. She has published many papers in reputed journals on varied themes, ranging from Dalit Literature to African and to Indian English Literature. She is in the Editorial Board of many Academic bodies.

Preeti Singh is Assistant Professor in the Department of English at Karamat Husain Muslim Girls' Postgraduate College, University of Lucknow, Lucknow. She has published many research papers in the reputed National and International Journals.

Rituparna Das is part-time lecturer in the Department of English at Rishi Bankim Chandra College, Naihati, West Bengal and a research scholar in the Department of English in the University of Calcutta. She is also a recipient of Rajiv Gandhi National Fellowship.

Samina Parvin is a research scholar in the Department of English, Aligarh Muslim University, Aligarh. She has many research papers to her credit.

Sarika Kanjlia is Assistant Professor in the Department of English at D.A.V. Centenary College, Faridabad Haryana. She has many research papers to her credit.

Shoaib Ekram is Assistant professor in the Department of English in English and Foreign Languages University (Central University), Hyderabad, Lucknow Campus. Presently he is working on Mahesh Dattani.

Soumyadip Ghosh is research scholar in the Department of English in the University of North Bengal. His areas of interest are Indian Drama in English and Postcolonial Theatre.

Tuhin Majumdar shares his knowledge as Assistant Professor in the Department of English in Khatra Adibasi Mahavidyalaya, Khatra, The University of Burdwan and has rendered his services as an Assistant Professor of English Language and Technical Communication in Hooghly Engineering and Technology College, Hooghly, Kolkata. Having completed his masters from Banaras Hindu University, Uttar Pradesh, he has cleared UGC-NET and (JRF) and is also pursuing Ph.D. in Graphic Novels from The University of Burdwan, West Bengal and has published many papers in peer-reviewed National and International Journals.

1

Brief Candle: Life in Death or Death in Life?

Neha Arora

> Out, out, brief candle!
> Life is but a walking shadow, a poor player
> That struts and frets his hour upon the stage
> And then is heard no more. It is a tale
> Told by an idiot, full of sound and fury,
> Signifying nothing. (*Macbeth*, Scene 5, Act 5, p. 120)

Centuries ago, the Bard of Avon thus defined 'life' and the same bleak thought runs down to the present age too. The 'outsider sensibility' of the twentieth century is aptly anticipated and projected by Shakespeare in the above lines. Power politics has led to the ebbing of humanity in the contemporary age which is primarily characterised by disillusionment, loneliness and alienation. The mad race after Mammon has murdered God, faith, love, Nature, leaving man stranded, questioning to himself: Who am I? Wandering aimlessly on earth, he has gone astray. Be it Camus' Absurdism, Sartre's Existentialism or Hemingway's Nada—all define the Nihilism that has seeped into the lives of modern man. Whether it be Sophocles' 'call no one happy until he is dead' (*Oedipus Rex*) or Arnold's 'we mortal millions live alone' or Hardy's 'happiness is an occasional episode in the general drama of pain' (*The Mayor of Casterbridge*) or Beckett's 'nothing happens, nobody comes, nobody goes, it's awful' (*Waiting for Godot*), the emotional barrenness of man is echoed at the highest crescendo. The irony is, we 'Yanks' have ourselves locked us in 'cages' of temporary pleasures and are now unable to break it.

Literature is replete with such horrifying image of modern humanity, groping in darkness. The writers have often identified the world with a stage with definite roles assigned to each actor; neither the entry nor the exit is in our control. However, the analogy can be interpreted in two opposite views: either to mourn throughout the performance, thinking about the impending end or to enjoy our part in the play, irrespective of the length of the role. It is here that Mahesh Dattani differs from Beckett or Arnold or Hardy, etc. He prefers to opt for the second option and hence, his plays too ooze with Browning's 'Robust Optimism'. With no sign of lamentation over the dying faith, his plays open our eyes to a more subtle reality—'there is no end before the real end'. And also the 'real end' is itself not an 'end', rather a phase that needs to be faced, lived and enjoyed. What Browning expounded in 'Rabbi Ben Ezra', Dattani seems to dramatize the same philosophy. It is through such themes that he has gained an international stature. The settings of his plays are metropolitan India; however, neither his themes nor his characters are restricted to India only. His philosophy of life comes wrapped in the simple language, spoken by his characters who are none other but common people like us and this quality lends universal colour to his plays. The USP of Dattani's plays is the ease with which he forges connection with his readers/ audience. Although his characters and subjects come from common masses, the treatment elevates him to the rank of one of the greatest dramatists of the world.

His recent play *Brief Candle* discusses the universal theme of life and death, its characters epitomise Tennyson's Ulysses' dictum: 'to strive, to seek, to find, and not to yield'. Horace Walpole well presented in his letter to Anne, Countess of Ossary that 'the world is a comedy to those who think; a tragedy to those that feel'. Similarly, despite suffering with the fatal disease of cancer, the characters in the play *Brief Candle* are not bogged down by the brutality of the painful truth and do not die before they are actually dead. Redefining 'life' and 'death', they reject the notion of 'death in life' and uphold the idea of 'life in death'. Through the indomitable will of his characters, Dattani projects and propounds the anti-Sisyphus stand. He changes the typical modern view of life as a punishment/burden; for him life is a journey with a purpose and should not be let go so easily; it is a duty that should be performed with utter sincerity. The motif of 'Cancer' used in the play does not imply the disease merely; extending the image further, it symbolises the harsh winds of various troubles that ravage our lives every moment. But the solution does not lie in fleeing them; 'escapism' is nowhere seconded by Dattani, either in this play or any other. He believes in confronting the problems instead of letting them overpower us. In *Brief Candle* the characters are all cancer patients in a hospital who are well aware of their destiny, yet are not ready to surrender to death. The 'candle' of life may be 'brief' but it still lightens the darkness of our world, hence, it should be respected. *Brief Candle* rejuvenates the dying faith in ourselves, it instils in us a respect towards the precious gift bestowed upon us by the Almighty. Thus, although a postmodern writer, Dattani's play is not a bundle of nihilism; the gloom of meaninglessness is countered by the spark of optimism. Vikas dies in the play, but only physically; spiritually and emotionally he always lives in the hearts of the characters because he had 'taught' them the *mantra* to stay alive until death finally detaches them from the physical world. The 'presence' of Vikas (Dattani deliberately does not uses the term 'ghost') is a postmodern approach to blur the fine line between life and death and to establish the fact that death is not a full stop, people do not die even in death. Vikas may not have been a successful medico, or a successful lover but he succeeded in achieving immortality (in the modern sense) by being able to see in the patients something 'more than just rotting trees' (*Brief Candle*, 25).Whether to perceive life as a feeble 'candle' or as a strong 'torch' is entirely an individual's perception. *Brief Candle* seems to echo Shaw's words:

> I want to be thoroughly used up when I die, for the harder I work, the more I live. I rejoice in life for its own sake. Life is no 'brief candle' for me. It is a sort of

> splendid torch, which I have got hold of for the moment; and I want to make it burn as brightly as possible before handing it on to future generations. (Kamath, *The Pursuit of Excellence*)

Dattani's oeuvre is evidence enough for his world-wide acclaim. His global readership is the upshot of his themes that are not local but universal. 'Powerful and disturbing', this is how D.J.R. Bruckner praises Mahesh Dattani in the *New York Times* and the words directly comment on the carefully chosen themes of the playwright. Dattani sets himself apart from his contemporaries by plunging into the lives of middle-class Indians and bringing them/their issues on the stage. *Brief Candle* centres on the patients who are in double pain—the agony of the disease and also the social stigma. Dattani portrays life from their angle, their fear of the society; he depicts that side of the story of which the rich people are completely ignorant. Shanti and Amarinder are worried because the disease has attacked their very identity. They are well aware of the fact that the Indian middle-class mentality castigates an infertile/incomplete woman and an impotent man and by losing one breast Shanti becomes a 'lesser woman' and Amarinder a 'lesser man', rather a eunuch.

For him, all issues are to be/should be in the mainstream and should be discussed openly. In *Brief Candle*, he chooses to unmask a section of people in India who do not have the courage to bear their disease because of the inhumane society. It is not the disease that kills them; it is the thoughts of the attitude of the narrow-minded conservative Indian society that gradually cripples them mentally. In his daring attempts of taking up the cause of eunuchs, homosexuals, HIV/AIDS patients, etc., Dattani's plays have received varied responses from the audience which is a blend of liberal and conservative mind sets.

As a prolific writer, Dattani dons many roles and feathers in his cap. A graduate in History, Political Science and Economics, and postgraduate in Marketing and Advertising Management, he had nothing, albeit directly, to do with art and literature until 1986 when he wrote his first full-length play *Where There's a Will*. From that time, his pen and his art have seen no full stop. As an actor, as director, as script writer, as dancer, the nouns would fall short in sketching a full-portrait of 'the man of the people'. Although there is no dearth of writers in India, what distinguishes Dattani from the rest is his ability to connect with the masses. Even in respect to the language, he very consciously chooses not the 'English' of the elite and sophisticated class but the 'english' of the educated urban middle-class Indians.

It is not that his characters are trapped in the complicated situations; he impels them to have a deeper insight to realize that it is actually 'we all' who are caught in the whirlpool of our complexities. He mirrors our own image. In the Preface to *Collected Plays*, he writes:

> I am certain that my plays are a true reflection of my time, place and socio-economic background. I am hugely excited and curious to know what the future holds for me and my art in the new millennium in a country that has a myriad challenges to face politically, socially, artistically and culturally. (2000: XV)

Virginia Woolf, in her essay "Mr Bennett and Mrs Brown" (1924) commented that 'on or around December 1910 human nature changed' and twentieth century or rather the closing decades of the nineteenth century shifted the focus of literature to the inner world of human life. The perpetual internal conflict provided loads of raw material to the writers to develop their thoughts and enabled them to see and also make the others see the bitter reality. Devices such as stream of consciousness, interior monologues, flashback, etc. were profusely used to keep the real, real. They did away with the artificiality of maintaining a façade before the audience. The reader/audience is no more external to the text/performance, s/he is as much an integral character as are the others. Italo Calvino's 'If on a Winter's Night a Traveller' explores the co-existence of reader/audience in the creation and development of a literary work. The traditional method of 'story telling' is passé, now the plot unfolds gradually and abruptly. Keeping up with the new literary style, Dattani also exploits several such devices.

In *Brief Candle*, each character has been given separate space, time and words enough to recall their past and relate the horrors of their lives which their disease has brought to them. The individual soliloquies are a clever insertion by the playwright to lend authenticity to their stories. The flashback technique brings together different time zones (the clock time and the time-in-mind) and this all the more emphasizes the psyche of the characters. It performs a kind of X-ray and serves the inner workings of the characters and brings their thoughts out for the audience. The shame and pain of the past and the struggle in the present enhance the agony of the characters. Amarinder recalls the day when his biopsy was made and he 'woke up feeling sore inside' (23), Shanti juxtaposes the hesitation of a newly-wed bride and her shock and pain of cancer and chemotherapy, Amol's desperation to be 'hidden' somewhere (the I spy game, 38)—this 'sore', 'shock', 'I spy/hiding' are indicative of how, human beings in reality, desperately attempt to avoid the unpleasant truths but all in vain. Confronting, and not evading is the solution to the problems.

'Masks' form an important technique in Dattani to lay thrust upon his themes. Also, it is very integral/natural to us who 24*7 are 'masked'. In *Final Solutions*, (there) was a mob wearing masks of two different communities, in *Brief Candle* the 'Face of Cancer' dominates the set and acts as a reader to the excruciating pain (physical/emotional/psychological) of the cancer patients. It is used as a motif by the characters who, one by one, lay bare their souls to the audience. The traditional soliloquies are replaced by the presence of this concrete 'face' that continuously tortures them, goads them to burst out their repressed feelings and provides a cathartic vent. As a postmodernist device, Dattani's 'Face of Cancer' becomes the pivot around which the entire drama is woven; in real life, it can come as the moments when individuals finally break down. In Scene III, the Face of Cancer is transformed into smaller masks which Vikas dangles in front of every character in turns and they reveal their stories one by one. Amarinder and Shanti are anxious about their bodily changes that would transform not just them but also the attitude of society towards them. They both share their apprehensions, whereas Deepika is constantly concealing her emotions for Vikas. Dattani carefully chooses the time to insert the grim reality in the web of fantasy. The 'visible mask' removes the 'invisible mask' from the actors and reveals the 'real' men and women. The light-hearted Amarinder recalls his first stay at the hospital and his fear of losing his 'maleness' (manhood):

> Amarinder: The biopsy was made and I woke up feeling sore inside.... They never told me that they will be drilling inside my body. At my core. What made me a man? Climbing a mountain, playing a game of hockey, knowing I could satisfy a woman in bed. All that was under attack with a group of needles probing at my prostate.... A gland the size of a walnut that defines my maleness. What will I choose? To live? And deal with the loss? Instead of vitality, flowing through my loins, bear embarrassment of urine dribbling down my pants and not even noticing it? I wanted to live! With everything I had! (*Brief Candle*, 23)

The mask of coquettish Unnikrishnan falls and the pain ridden Shanti takes over:

> Shanti: Our maid showed me the blood stains on my brassiere. She thought I had hurt myself. She told my mother-in-law. She insisted, 'I go for a test...I lay exposed to the technicians, my breast pushed against the X-ray plate. One of them marked my lumps, treating my breast as if it were already a piece of dead flesh.... At least I could say no to Mukund, but the doctors, lab technicians.... Their job was to invade my body and take out tumours, and they did. But they grew and came back till they took it all out. A part of me that I had barely felt. That I had never seen fully myself. Gone. (*Brief Candle*, 32)

Again there is a blend of reality and fiction in the character of Amol Sengupta who would not be allowed to stay the next night in the hotel as he had exceeded his credit card limit, and Amol the actor/real had run out of money, hence, his treatment could not continue in the hospital (38). The fine line dividing fantasy and reality blurs away and this intermixing of reality with the imaginary accentuates the pain of a patient who is left maimed for life, physically cured but emotionally and psychologically mutilated. Wearing the masks of pretentions, human beings try to evade reality throughout their lives but like the 'Face of Cancer' challenges keep hovering upon us. By closing our eyes, we cannot but befool ourselves; Dattani's actors/characters pouring out is the method of accepting the truth. Dattani does not aim for Aristotelian catharsis, his intention is even larger—not escapism but only confrontation with the reality.

The play *Brief Candle* is set in a hospital and the actors are the survivors of cancer. They are rehearsing a play to be performed as a fundraiser for their hospice. The writer of the play (within-the-play) Vikas, was also one of them but he had died of cancer. The audience confronts with a play-within-play in the very beginning but unlike other examples of this device, Dattani juxtaposes the past and the present such that the readers/audience need to be on their toes always to identify when and where the reel merges with the real. He does not narrate the past incidents; rather it is only through the conversation among the characters that much of the reality is unfolded. Dattani, the playwright has created Vikas, the dramatist. Vikas knows about the past (and also present) lives of the actors and the dialogues exchanged between the characters are directly taken from the actors' real lives. For example, when Mahesh is told by Deepika to stay and share a room for a night with Mr. Sengupta, he is irritated to the extent of saying "Arre, what will you know? In Kolhapur they clear the runway for my private plane" (*Brief Candle*, 7). For the characters, actors and audience, it is merely a conversation between the two characters. But only the dramatist, Vikas and the actor Mahesh know that this was something shared by latter with him. It was Mahesh's (the ward boy's) desire to become a rich man that was moulded and presented by Vikas in his script. Amarinder was scared of losing his 'manhood', he plays a man desperately in 'need' of Miss Unnikrishnan; Mahesh (the ward boy) was inclined towards Deepika; he acts as Mr. Sengupta, ready to seduce Deepika, the receptionist; Amol is Mr. Sengupta who is running out of cash, hence, can no longer stay in the hotel whereas in reality it was due to the financial crisis that his treatment at the hospital was to be stopped. So the script of the play-within-the-play is framed on the real lives of the actors and the information is interspersed in the dialogues of the characters. Thus, the words exchanged by the characters give a glimpse to the world of the actors. Dattani has very intelligently blended the reel with the real. Vikas is omnipresent and the characters share a very transparent relationship with him. He can be interpreted/perceived as the concretized form of our abstract conscience. Human beings may wear various masks and take up pretentions, but to their conscience they are always bare, from it they can never escape—the conscience knows our desires, our fears, as did Vikas.

Dattani prefers to use composite sets. Like in *Tara* in *Brief Candle* also, he divides the entire stage space into various 'levels', with action going on in each, simultaneously. The use of 'split stage' is a favourite device used repeatedly by Dattani. In *Tara* the technique helps in accentuating the agony of Chandan (Dan); *Brief Candle* opens in a room with Deepika, Mahesh and Mr. Kulkarni, we can also see Vikas 'on a high level or at the top of the face' (7) and Shanti 'dancing to herself in the shower' (13) when the other characters were busy in their conversations. The use of split stage saves time on one hand, on the other it also stresses the realistic element. Split stage also coincides with the various incidents and emotions that go on simultaneously in our lives, the lips have to bear a smile even though the eyes are wet. As against the conventional dramas, nothing escapes the postmodern audience. Dattani exploits the montage technique of contemporary times and this juxtaposition also aids in accelerating the tempo of the play. His stage is almost barren, devoid of the gaudy decor. Instead his idea is to keep it as natural as it can be. Scene I opens in a hotel room which is just a room in the hospital. The most conspicuous of all is the large 'Face of Cancer', a three-dimensional 'androgynous face' that is 'melting': 'Hollow eyes, sallow skin, tufts of hair, etc. A face that is ravaged by the effects of chemotherapy and is now ready to give up the struggle' (*Brief Candle*, 7). As in his other dramas, here, too he uses 'a composite set' with a 'gauze curtain' to separate the spaces. In no manner he attempts to follow the traditional dramatists who created an illusion around their audience. Dattani's audience is very much a part of his drama and is witness to everything happening on and behind the stage.

The modern urban Indian people have removed the veil of conventional modesty, hence Dattani's characters too unabashedly talk about sex and other taboo subjects. He does not shy away from using candid language and also pun. In an age that has marched ahead all the taboos, he drops the façade of modesty and profusely uses Freudian slips to heighten the modernity and candidness of the present society. Sexual connotations are freely sprinkled in *Brief Candle* too. Amarinder Malhotra is interested to be 'hooked up' for a night with Miss Unnikrishnan (played by Shanti), Mahesh seems to be interested in Deepika and flirts with her convincing that for her he could do anything, Deepika, on the other hand, is like any modern girl who dallies in coquetry now and then. Amarinder freely asks Mahesh for a 'Viagra pill' to prove to Miss Unnikrishnan 'how good I am in.... How good I am at.... You know—a real man' (*Brief Candle*, 11), then there is Miss Unnikrishnan who could be seen 'brushing her hair singing a Hindi film song *paani mein jale, paani mein jale mera gora badan...*' (*Brief Candle*, 28).

However, one should not overlook the relevance of such connotations. Beneath the veneer of physicality lies Dattani's philosophy. On one such light flirtatious and intimate moment between Amarinder and Shanti, the strap of her innerwear breaks and she is left half naked in the top. Although one may find breaking of Unnikrishnan's strap and covering her 'left breast with a towel' titillating, it is here that the agony of Shanti is misinterpreted to be the sensuality of Unnikrishnan. When 'unintentionally the towel slips off' her breast, it is not Unnikrishnan who feels embarrassed, but Shanti who breaks down, it is not Amarinder the lustful man who utters 'Oh my God!', but the real Amarinder who is reminded of his own pain seeing Shanti in that condition. Dattani blends perfectly the fun and pathos (a typical feature of the theatre of Absurd) leaving the audience gaping. The truth was that Shanti did not have the left breast as a result of numerous chemotherapy sessions and Amarinder too was suffering from prostate cancer. However, the difference was whereas, Shanti could accept her fate, Amarinder was in dilemma, 'whether I choose not to have the surgery and die. Or live without really living' (*Brief Candle*, 33). Shanti's 'acceptance of her fate' does not imply her passivity; she does not surrender to the doings of her disease; in fact acting cowardly, Amarinder tried to put off the surgery fearing the loss of his manhood in the future but his present is not all pleasant. The rationality lies in facing the reality, not running from it. The unseen future seems to be dearer to the human beings that they readily forego the comfort of the present, and by continuously going back to the peaceful past, the agony gets all the more aggravated, rightly put by Tennyson in *Locksley Hall* as 'That a sorrow's crown of sorrow is remembering happier things' (76). The Cavalier motto of 'Eat, drink and be merry, for tomorrow ye die' seems to have been lost in the pages of history.

The existential element is very much found in the ironic name given to the hotel 'Hotel Staylonger', a place where they have taken refuge only for a night. The name of the hotel is very apt—'Staylonger'—everyone wants to stay longer in the world, forgetting that the world is but a hotel for us and not a permanent abode, we are the 'guests', not 'residents'. Amol's intervention is quite significant in extending the existential theme and emphasising upon the uncertainty of the future: "Ah, but we don't know when we are flying. Tomorrow, day after, or never" (*Brief Candle*, 10). The metaphor of arrival, departure, stay, staylonger—tell very appropriately remind us the essence of life—that is uncertain, uneven, what will happen the next moment but ignoring all these obstructions the journey of life goes on. Not the number of years, rather the quality of our lives is important and this is the thrust of the play, the brief time in this world is emphasized between arrival (birth) and departure (death). Many years ago, Rabindranath Tagore delineated with the similar issue in his play *The Post Office*. His Amol keeps on 'waiting' for a letter from the King in the same way as Beckett's Estragon and Vladimir 'wait' for Godot. The act of 'waiting' is quite significant—it implies doing nothing and yet doing something. 'Hope' and 'belief' are the oars for the boat of life to propel further, without them the boat will capsize. Vikas reveals this eternal truth to his fellow patients who remain indebted to him forever. Despite all odds, he had lived his life to the fullest and counsels the same to the other patients. There is no regret in him, but only music. The play introduces him sitting on a 'high level or at the top of the face' with 'a keyboard that he plays in different modes' (*Brief Candle*, 7). His first appearance is itself symbolical of adjusting/adapting/moulding himself according to the situation. Music runs perennially in the play. It symbolises the rhythm of life—again it is entirely upon us whether to make a cacophony of melody or vice versa.

Without being didactic, Dattani manages to sensitize his people of the gravity of the subject. *Brief Candle* cleverly exposes the hypocritical norms of the Indian society. A woman without her breast and a man sans his sexual ability are ostracised. A person who is already suffering with illness is tortured by the hollow codes. It encapsulates the dejection of a dying man, the degeneration of modern man and also the struggle against death. Dattani's experimentalist style blends the pessimism and existentialism of twentieth century with the life-affirming values in the otherwise dead people. Both, the setting of the play as well as the characters, it seems, have deliberately been chosen to slap hard in the face of pessimism. The play is set in a hospital ward and the actors are the terminally ill patients, but their show (their performance), their energy is an answer to their ill-fated dark future. The play is essentially modern in theme as it contains the seeds of 'hope' against their definite end and is postmodern in techniques/devices employed by Dattani. The play-within-the-play, the division of the stage at various levels, the perennial hanging of a character who is dead, the conversation with the dead, the juxtaposition of time, the flashback, etc. all contribute in making the play essentially Dattani. The subtitle of the play "A Dance between Love and Death" complements the title in justifying the significance of the flickering of the candle, until it finally extinguishes. The play carries the philosophical implication of life and death. The thread of existentialism runs through all his plays. With no idea of moralizing, Dattani philosophizes upon the essence of life, what makes life worthy of and also the significance of death. His *Brief Candle* is an exemplary of the same. The motif of selection of elements like cancer, hospital, pain, struggle, desire to live, etc. for the setting of the play, help in constructing the image of 'life' surrounded by unnumbered thorny problems and natural calamities. 'Hospital' could be interpreted as the mortal world where 'patients'/ people come to be cured of their ailments and can meet both life and death face to face. In life they suffer with the 'Cancer' of problems and struggle hard to swim against the tide. 'Hospital' could also mean the physical world and the 'patients' symbolise imperfect human beings with their deformities/limitations. The successful 'performance' will result from teamwork, also with the internal character and external character becoming one. But only those who understand the *mantra* of confronting with the reality manage to overcome the obstacles and live on like Vikas in the play. Even Vikas could be the metaphysical symbol of our lives. Until Deepika was avoiding accepting him, he kept coming back, but only when finally she does acknowledge his presence (47) that he could die in peace. Vikas is our inner fear, also the dark truth that we keep rejecting, fooling none other but ourselves.

There is a continuous oscillation between past and present and a very fine line divides them (if at all), otherwise, usually the two time periods overlap. In Scene IV too, while playing Miss Unnikrishnan and Amarinder, unintentionally the towel drops from Shanti's breasts, leaving Amarinder in shock and Shanti in tears, only Deepika was composed. She, as a doctor, fails to penetrate deep into the pain beyond a certain limit. For her, pain is just physical whereas the sociological trauma and psychological agony connects the patients. Amarinder was able to understand Shanti's tears as he himself was devoid of the organ that defined his manhood (as was with Shanti). It is the common agony that brings the two actors closer.

Adopting the device of 'foreshadowing', the conclusion of Scene I takes us into the past of Vikas and Deepika's life when they both were together in some medical college, in Scene II we are transported to the immediate past when Vikas was alive but the relationship between him and Deepika was that of a patient and doctor. The Garcian element of Magic Realism could be sensed in the perennial presence of the dead Vikas. He has penetrated in the life of each patient, "Mahesh: He is not absent! He does not want to go! He is clinging on! To us!" (27). The rehearsal is abruptly brought to an end in Scene I by Deepika who seemed disturbed by a phone call—which was of the dead Vikas, followed by a conversation between 'Doctor' Deepika and 'dead' Vikas. Although he is no more, his presence is always felt by everyone, but in different manner. For Deepika, it was a past she seems to running away from but it keeps haunting her like a nightmare. However, it is apparent that all is not dead in their hearts, especially Vikas, who drops a hint that he 'will touch you with this play of mine. From the dead. Mortmain'. (*Brief Candle*, 16).

Directed by Lillette Dubey, *Brief Candle* was first performed on the 5th of July, 2009 at Mumbai by the Prime Time Theatre Company and published by Penguin in 2010. The playsings that pain, tragedy, suffering and death are inescapable in human life. The promos of *Brief Candle* described it as:

> A play that addresses mortality yet highlights life that emphasises the importance of the quality of our lives rather than how long we live it. The play is a hilarious farce with some extremely funny situations revolving around a hotel room near the airport. As the characters in the play await their departures, which are delayed due to a storm, they end up in comic situations, as they entangle themselves in surreptitious dalliances and complicated love affairs. (Drama Dose for Theatre Junkies: Sep. 6 2009)

There is love, romance, sex, comedy, tragedy, philosophy; all blended together to design "a brief candle" which brings the people closer to real life. The single line, 'that's what I needed. Just a touch' (*Brief Candle*, 18) spoken by Vikas summarises the play which is all about life, about death and how to live death rather than dying life. Through Vikas, a second life was infused in the otherwise dead people. One is reminded of the vivacious Anand of the famous Bollywood movie *Anand*. Despite knowing that the end was near, he taught the people to accept the loss but continue to live until the last breath. Be it Amarinder or Shanti, Mahesh or Amol, Vikas taught them the real meaning of life and counselled them to accept the thorns too in the bed of roses (*Brief Candle*, 23). He helped them to see the light of hope in the dark tunnels of their illness. The play is about compassion, the love/concern the 'patients' require.

Something similar is dealt by Dattani in his 'Ek Alag Mausam' that centres around the AIDS patients. On one hand are the patients who are 'like a rotting tree that is about to fall' (*Brief Candle*, 25), and on the other, are the doctors who 'are interested in the tree only till the rot is removed' (*Brief Candle*, 25), irrespective of something essential they require beyond medication. However, it should not be deduced that Dattani aims at creating any rift between the doctors and the patients. The play should be read as something that helps us in rising above the mortal clinging, that lends a hand to us in seeing, accepting and correcting our failures. It is a typical modern play where Vikas tries to imbue some hope in the otherwise dejected lot, to light a candle, although briefly, but teaches them to respect life. He pulls them out of the darkness of fear that engulfed them completely. He makes them face reality, with confidence and without guilt/shame/embarrassment.

> Shanti: But I saw Amar. I saw Fear. The same fear that I had. It wasn't the fear of death. It was the fear of....
>
> Amarinder: It was the fear—that....
>
> Vikas: It is the fear of losing something that you have and did not even think of the possibility of not having. But now when there is a real danger of losing it, you begin to understand its true worth. And then you are afraid you will have to live without it for the rest of your living moments. (*Brief Candle*, 24)

The crux of the play is revealed by Deepika, "This play also shows, to all of us here, that all of us have a right to live as long as we can and to laugh at our own follies" (*Brief Candle*, 47) and this is what Dattani aimed at. A candle, however, almost at the verge extinguishing, could not/should not be ignored. Till it is serving the purpose and giving light, its existence matters. Life too should be lived with gusto, not to be taken as a burden. The meaning is inherent in the way life is lived. Dattani's *Brief*

Candle is anti-nihilistic, anti-Shakespearean belief; for him "life is not a tale told by an idiot signifying nothing", it is a cluster of interconnected moments put together which signify everything. Even though the human existence on the stage of physical world is transitory, its significance cannot be ignored. It concretises Browning's 'to strive and to yield not, that's the spirit'.

Works Cited

Chakraborty, Kaustav. *Indian Drama in English*. New Delhi: PHI Pvt. Ltd., 2011. Print.

Chaudhuri, Asha Kuthari. *Contemporary Indian Writers in English: Mahesh Dattani*. New Delhi: Cambridge University Press, 2008. Print.

Das, Bijay Kumar. *Forms and Meaning in Mahesh Dattani's Plays*. New Delhi: Atlantic Publishers, 2008. Print.

Dattani, Mahesh. Preface to *Collected Plays*. New Delhi: Penguin Books India Pvt. Ltd., 1994. Print.

——. *Brief Candle*. New Delhi: Penguin Books India, 2010.

"Drama Dose for Theatre Junkies". Sep 6 2009. <http://www.dramadose.com/brief-candle/> Web.

Kamath, M.V. *The Pursuit of Excellence*. New Delhi: Rupa & Co., 2000. Print.

Konar, Ankur. "Drama, Dattani and Discourse: Position and Exposition" in *Lapiz Lazuli: An International Literature Journal*, Vol. 2, No. 2, Autumn 2012. Print.

McRae, John. "A Note on the Play *On a Muggy Night in Mumbai*" in *Collected Plays Mahesh Dattani*. Penguin, 2000, 45. Print.

Mee, Erin B. "Contemporary Indian Theatre: Three Voices": 4. *PAJ*. Vol. 19, Jan 1997. 1-5. Print.

——. "Mahesh Dattani: Invisible Issues" in *Performing Arts Journal*. PAJ, Inc. Vol. 19, No. 1, Jan. 1997, p. 19. <http: www.jstor.org/stable/3245741>. Accessed on 06/06/2014. Web.

Mukherjee, Tutun. "I Do Not Write Merely to be Read". *The Hindu*, <http://www.hinduonnet.com/thehindu/mp/2004/07/26/stories/2004072601790100.htm>

Nair, Anita. "Mahesh Dattani—The Invisible Observer". www.anitanair.net/profiles/profile-m-d.html.

Shakespeare, William. *Macbeth*. E-book. www.feedbooks.com. Web.

Velmani, N. *Drama in Indian Writing in English—Tradition and Modernity*. Vol. 13:6, June 2013:16. Web.

2

Postmodernism in Dattani's *Where There is a Will*

Bishun Kumar

With his experimentalist and expressionist technique in theatre studies, Mahesh Dattani has emerged as a 'morning star' in the history of play-writing in India. His plays are experimentation of human psyche with varying social, educational and political situation. He is dramatist of the contemporary world that is free from religious, communal, regional and national boundaries. Almost all his plays have universal appeal of contemporary human nature, his sentiments and his existential problems. Dattani is a close observer of contemporary human life rather than blind believer of old set patterns of life. He thus, succeeds in liberating man from the clutches of meaningless customs, tradition and mythical beliefs. He, then questions the historical view of life for he does not find it suitable in current rapidly changing scenario. The themes, issues and subject matter incorporated in his plays prepare the ground for evolving a new theory, the theory experimentable in contemporary life of man. The process of novelization in plots, themes and techniques of drama does not mean that he has entirely subverted the values of ancient myths, concepts, theories, traditions and customs. Dattani, as an experimentalist into life, successfully filters the good, the valuable without ignoring the evil—a binary opposite but a complementary and counterpart of life. He, however with essential modifications, makes it suitable for the contemporary conditions of human life what we call 'love to innovation' to make life full of pleasures and happiness and to balance the equation of human existentialism.

The epistemological view of life that began in mid 17th century in modern age and continued till 20th century though with situational modifications but always devoted to 'power as reason'—the enlightenment to improve human society as evidenced in (a) 18th century—an age of reason (b) 19th century—French revolution and ended in (c) 20th century—lament on loss for reason. Such ideas are expressed/embodied in the philosophy of Kant in Germany, Voltaire and Diderot in France, Lock and Hulme in Britain. The period of 1950 and after realized the break with these modernist traditions. Consequently blind faith in traditions, set patterns and slavish obedience to religious precepts and prohibitions were transferred/replaced by 'faith in reason' and the 'existential problems' as well. This change in human attitude registers the advent of new avant-garde, i.e. post-modernism. Linda Hutcheon distinguishes postmodernism from modernism telling fact that it "takes the form of self-conscious, self-contradictory, self-undermining statement" (*Politics*, 1988: 1). One way of creating this double or contradictory stance on any statement is the use of parody: citing a convention only to make fun of it. As Hutcheon explains, "Parody—often called ironic quotation, pastiche, appropriation, or intertextuality—is usually considered central to postmodernism, both by its detractors and its defenders" (*Politics*, 1988: 93). And Dattani's play *Where There is a Will* is a parody of a neo-capitalist man.

As Marxist critic Walter Benjamin once stated with remarkable perspicuity, "There is no document of civilization which is not at the same time a document of barbarism" (1992: 248). Thus, for the most part, humankind as a race and as an individual finds itself emerged in the ambiguous grey zone of judgment in which right or wrong, good and evil, civilization and barbarism, lease to exist in a tidy binary opposition, as distinctions between them become blurred and confused in a series of complex interrelationship, a grey zone both lived and explored by Holocaust survivor Primo Levi, who argued that, "compassion and brutality can coexist in the same individual and in the same moment, despite all logic" (1994: 29). Like blurred images evincing many interpretations at the same time, blending of concepts, theories, and ideas is a significant feature of postmodernist writing.

In his plays, Dattani blends ancient with modern, classical with contemporary, myth with realism, religion with industrialism, good with evil, pleasant with unpleasant and so many other binaries. This, on the one hand, links the opposites as a complementary part of the whole and on the other hand, it (postmodernism) claims that no man, concept, theory, or philosophy is pure, rather every aspect of life is bewildered may be in odd or even ratio what critics have recognized in the name of a variety of literary techniques like intertextuality, parody, pastiche, metaphor and allegory, etc.

Dattani's rejection of Aristotelian parameter of Drama (such as time dimension and the three unities) portrays his love for portraying segmented realities or acceptance for segmented facts of life, the truth in bits and bytes and individual experiences rather than man as a complete being. His theory of Drama rejects the portrayal of ideal life, the good or even the poetic justice the very feature of ancient theatre presents the polarized human facts between high and low, ideal and mean, general and individual existing at the same time in a single being which is the very essence of postmodernism. As Peter Barry says, "The modernist lament fragmentation while postmodernists celebrate it" (*Beginning Theory*, 2002: 85). Dattani's plays revolve round Peter Barry's remark:

> Postmodernism rejects the difference between 'high' and 'popular' art which was important in modernism and believes in excess, in gaudiness, and in 'bad taste' mixture of qualities. (*Beginning Theory*, 2002: 85)

Postmodernism is neither a theory nor a philosophy but a mode of presentation that focuses on ontological view of life. There are certain hidden realities in the society for which there is no proper reasoning, no concept, no philosophy of life which could be applicable on such wizard realities but the truth is that they do exist. The facts like homosexuality, alternative sexuality, lesbian relationship, incest, child sexual abuse and bisexual nature of man are not features of a cultured life (sociological aspects of culture) therefore all are taken derogatively in the society and regarded as taboos and sinful acts. No writer of idealist attitude, except Dattani dares to write on these social realities and if anyone could he treated it derogatively and in humiliating manner instead experimenting the physical, biological, psychological and social factors working as a turbulent misguiding force. But Dattani's play *Tara* (1990) deals with bisexual nature of man in form of Siamese Twins, and how one side of physical feature/nature is suppressed to hide and to be proud of unisexual while Dattani's play focuses on the "bisexuality is the essence of sexual pleasure" for Dattani himself tells that:

> Tara is about Siamese Twins who've been conjoined from the chest down, and I've taken the liberty of making them boy and girl twins. I think it's a play about the self, about the man and the woman in self, but a lot of people think of it as a play about the girl child. (Dattani in Interview with Erin B. Mee, *PAJ*, 1997)

His play *Dance Like a Man* (1989) deals with hollow ego of the patriarchal vigour and hierarchical code of conduct that does not permit a farther to allow his son to learn Bharatnatyam. That results in suppressing the natural instinct of dance in a boy Jairaj.

Availing fantasy to one's natural instinct gives immense pleasure to the being. Dattani's *Do the Needful* deals with the suppression of the instinct of homosexuality inherent in a character Alpesh. Only because of family prestige the turbulent desire of Alpesh is ignored but the playwright presents the deconstructed view of the heterosexuality reconstructing the relation of homosexuality. All these plays conclude against the expectations of traditional audience that is still in the grip of middle-class morality. But Dattani gives full opportunity to his characters to enjoy life to its fullest by fulfilling their natural desires that makes audience soul searching. For him the pleasures of life are the success of life. As believes Sita Raina, the Delhi-based actress and theatre director:

> Joy is the essence of life and I have always believed that theatre should exude delight. *Where There is a Will* is such a play. It is not only thought provoking and introspective but also provides an evening of pure entertainment. (A note on the play, *Where There is a Will*, 451)

It is for the sake of this 'joy' all set patterns, myths, concepts, theories that retard the naturalness of a being and hinder the ecstasy of life are subverted and perverted what is regarded as postmodernist view of life. The present paper will attempt at exploring postmodern realities in Dattani's drawing room comedy *Where There is a Will.* "Post modernism cannot be defined chronologically, but should rather be seen as a mode of representation present in every epoch", argues Umberto Eco commenting on his best selling medieval mystery novel, *The Name of the Rose.* As an aesthetic practice, a cultural epoch or a philosophy, it is plural, fluid, and open as against singular, rigid, fixed and close nature of the classical genres and concepts. Postmodernism is loose, flexible, and contingent. Dattani's play *Where There is a Will* captures all these features of postmodernity.

The play *Where There is a Will* is comedy of very serious social and familial issues such as family culture, obedience to the family head, power of control, husband-wife conflicts, extra-marital sex and degradation of females even in the end of 20th century. The play opens with a leading character Hasmukh Mehta in his drawing room conflicting with his son Ajit who seems taking decisions against his father's will. Hasmukh is waiting for his business call but is irritated because Ajit has engaged the phone. Ajit's wife Preeti crosses the room and appears to be busy in cooking. While smoking anxiously, Hasmukh asks frequently Preeti whether dinner is ready. Every time she answers is in affirmation. Through the conversation of Hasmukh with his son Ajit it is evident that he is swelled up with ego of his boss stature and ownership of company and the house as well. He had a deprived childhood for he had devoted himself to total obedience to his father. He did what his father wanted to and he wants the same from his son Ajit to obey him/ his orders. But Ajit wishes to live the life of his own, all free from his father's conditions. Through the speeches of his wife Sonal, we come to know that her husband Hasmukh Mehta is suffering from diabetes and surviving on the anti-diabetic pills. She has prepared *halwa* that both Hasmukh and Ajit like very much. But she too is guided by her sister Minal who has strictly forbidden giving sweets to Hasmukh. Therefore, she prepares *parathas* and salad for him. After dinner Hasmukh lies down in the sofa and dies.

In act II, Hasmukh acts as his own spirit happy of the Will he made and feels free from all his diseases. The Will reads that Hasmukh has given his property to trust making Kiran Jhaberi its trustee. Kiran Jhaberi is Managing director of the company and with whom Hasmukh had sexual relation too. The Will dictates the powers of Hasmukh even after his death that Aju will bear the office punctually and Kiran will control the office and his home as simultaneously.

Exploring the first feature of postmodernism in Dattani's play that is break with tradition, we notice that the playwright himself has broken with classical dramatic tradition be it Sanskrit Drama/Indian classical theatre or Greek theatre. He presents the truth inherent in contemporary modern society. He deviates from all the formal properties of drama including theme, plot, technique and subject matter. Dattani's objective seems not to tell why (the reason) but what happens in the society. It does happen in the society. Lyotard writes in this connection, "the status of knowledge is altered as societies enter what is known as the post-industrial age and cultures enter what is known as the post-modern age" (Lyotard, 1992: 3).

The prominent tools of postmodernist thinkers are skepticism, doubt and paranoia. A postmodernist usually believes that agreement is always enforced, that truth is merely coerced consensus, and everything is relative. Thus, we can move towards a more democratic mind-set only through a spirit of dispenses, a tolerance for difference, a move to the marginal, and through small, localized resistance. In a nut shell, instead of forcing once truth on someone, one should accept that they have their own story to tell.

The playwright Dattani, as a postmodernist thinker, does not agree with father's paramountcy/dictatorship in professional or private affairs of life; the dictates made by him will not be true for everyone. In the very opening of the play Ajit does not agree with his own father Hasmukh:

> Ajit: After all I am the Joint Managing Director.
>
> Hasmukh: Believe me, appointing him as the JMD was a big mistake.
>
> Ajit: And after all, I am his son....
>
> Hasmukh: That was an even bigger mistake. What makes it worse is knowing that I actually prayed to get him. Oh God! I regret it all please let him drop dead. No, no. ...ever since he entered my factory, he has been in my way.
>
> (Dattani. Act 1, *Where There is a Will* in *Collected Plays*, 2000: 456)

Both Ajit and his father are worried about the development of the company. Both have made their plans and projects. But the truth is that neither of them agrees to the other's project. In Ajit's opinion his father's ways are out dated, not suitable for contemporary modern society. In Hasmukh's opinion his son Ajit is inexperienced. His innovative new techniques will bring company to bankruptcy. He is experienced and his ways are proven for he has raised his company on his own plans/methods. On individual level both are true but together they are opposing each other.

The second feature the Postmodernism is that it attacks the idea of a stable, autonomous being, subvert the authority and the possibility of grounding our knowledge in certainty and truth. Dattani's leading character in *Where There is a Will,* Hasmukh as a skeptic, does not believe in his son Ajit and in his project enhancing the company will be true or worthwhile. He, therefore, makes a "Will"—a legal document to be acted upon, binding Ajit to play him after his death the way he himself played his father. He wants his working process to be stable he listens to none exercising his own autonomy in the organization. He does not even believe his mistress and trustee Kiran Jhaberi. In his Will, he has his own dictates to force her plans on her. After Hasmukh's death, as per guidelines of the Will, when she comes to live at his home the truth is revealed through her speeches. She herself attacks on his autonomy exercised through his Will. In one of the remarks made by Sonal, she tells:

> Kiran: .... Thank God, he was too drunk to impose himself on us; yes, Mrs. Mehta. My father, your husband, they were weak men with false strength.
>
> Hasmukh: What do you mean? How dare you compare me to your drunkard father?
>
> Kiran: Hasmukh was intoxicated with his power. He thought he was invincible. That he could rule from his grave by making this Will.
>
> (Dattani. *Where There is a Will* in *Collected Plays,* Act II. 2000: 456)

Images blurred with the traditional reality is the third feature of the postmodernism. Though, both the authority and its subjects are binary opposites and in a cultured society both 'dependence' and 'free will' emerge in their binaries but in the play *Where There is a Will* this distinction is blurred. In Act I, Hasmukh's communication with his family members portrays him of a 'free will' as 'a ruler' in making decisions, everyone has to obey him as he himself announces, "Hasmukh: You have the right to listen to my advice and obey my orders" (2000: 458). When in Act II his Will is exposed to us it seems that really he has won; he is the ruler. But while discussing with Sonal, Kiran discloses the secrets of his authority and power of decision making. Kiran tells:

> Kiran: He depended on me for everything. He thought he was the decision maker. But I was.... He wanted me to run his life. Like his father had. (Pause). Hasmukh did not really want a mistress. He wanted a father. He saw in me a woman who would father him! (Laughs. Hasmukh cringes at her laughter). Men never really grow up. (Dattani. *Collected Plays*, 2000: 510)

Kiran's above remark not only subverts the patriarchal dominance but also discloses radical feminist in her. Hutcheon suggests that postmodernism works through **parody** to "both legitimize and subvert that which it parodies" (*Politics*, 1988: 101). A woman controlling the actions of a man is a postmodern reality. Hasmukh, who stands himself a biggest capitalist hierarch, seems helpless in front of Kiran's power of decision making. Appearance of Will in Act II of the play is the most effective and binding tool of a capitalist like Hasmukh for power control. He is proud of his riches which he assumes the tool for exercising power. In a dramatic Monologue, he boasts of his affluence:

> .... I Hasmukh Mehta, am one of the richest men in this city. All by my own efforts. Forty-five years old and I am success in capital letters. Twenty-three years old and he is on the road to failure in bold capital letters! At his age, I was a mature responsible man, not eating my father's head and nibbling at papads! (Dattani. *Collected Plays,* 2000: 464)

Dattani reveals the hollowness of Hasmukh's personality through employment of the technique of asides. In his speeches, Hasmukh unconsciously uses the word 'father' frequently though to express proud of him but the fact is he himself is the shadow of his father. The father is locked in his unconscious. All his activities are guided by his father and not by the prevalent current situations and contemporary needs. He likes Kiran for her genius and courage of decision-making. She is bold, prudent and diligent in all her business dealings. He himself admits, she is, "Not an ordinary typist or even a secretary. A shrewd hard-headed marketing executive. If there was any one in my office who has brains to match mine, it was her" (Dattani. 2000: 473). He, thus, is overshadowed by Kiran's personality, talent, confidence and more especially an ability to read Hasmukh's psyche. When she starts executing his Will, she dwarfs his ideology of power control over herself and over his own family members.

One after one she discloses the hidden truths of Hasmukh Mehta; her revelation that he did not keep her as his mistress rather he found her a father figure who could always guide her. Hasmukh himself regrets that for 25 years he had had no sexual relationship with Sonal. For he finds her good-for-nothing and says, "Twenty-five years of marriage and I haven't enjoyed sex with her" (Dattani. 2000: 473). Though he boasts of his money that he could afford everything (life, personality, power, business and luxury life) with his money as he tells, "I could afford, those expensive ladies of the night in five star hotels! And what about my sex life? Well, I could afford that too" (2000: 473) but Kiran's statement that, "he did not want a mistress but a figure who could father him" discloses his physical vacuity too. In this way Hasmukh is a complex figure. He can neither be called good nor bad for what he does is not to torture anyone (Ajit, Preeti and Sonal) but to train them to be fit for business dealings and maintain harmony in familial relations. By intention he is an honest person but unfortunately he himself could not understand his own life and assumes himself to be the most intelligent. The dramatist has very brilliantly presented his mental and physical vacuity through his Will, asides and soliloquies. In his attempt to control his daughter-in-law Preeti and his wife Sonal, however, not to punish them but to domesticate them he himself is controlled by a woman like Kiran. Kiran, a woman whom he thought, presumably his slave, legally his trustee, practically she appears owner of him and his family. Thus, Hasmukh is a postmodern figure, the true representative of post-industrial society.

Unpredictability and multilevel personality of the contemporary man is yet another feature of postmodernism. Kiran Jhaberi whose personality is revealed as mistress of Hasmukh Mehta appointed as a typist and secretary of Mr. Mehta is a Managing Director from behind the curtains. During Hasmukh's life she appears to be very obedient and submissive but after his death she is seen very powerful. To be a mistress of a man is quite derogatory for an ideal woman in the society but when she appears on the stage, her character emerges to be a brilliant, honest, diligent and a pure woman like Tess of the D'Urbervilles, for, the relation that she develops with Sonal and Preeti is purely humanist. She, instead of dominating them, negotiates their weaknesses to leave them soul searching. Undoubtedly, some critics may charge her of sorority but at the same time they cannot ignore her for her visionary aspect of human relations. She balances both her home and her office as an expert Managing Director. She does her house hold duties by her own yet she never delays in performing the office responsibilities. She, in her multidimensional personality, appears as a postmodern woman deconstructing and subverting all traditional norms prevalent for women.

Her expertise at office is no less than an experienced and prudent man and her home management is no less than an ideal woman. Despite these two responsibilities she has always observed the third one that is to satisfy Hasmukh's erotic pleasures, not by surrendering herself in the hands of a puppet, a fool like Hasmukh but by having maintained her physique, the sensual appeal, the very fascination for men. This was a crucial part of her working mechanism. It could win her stability of her job over-taking the risk zone from where she could give "a free play" to her brains and spontaneity to her decision-making.

Kiran Jhaberi, thus, is not a woman figure but a composite figure of a successful executive, an ideal woman bridging both with a beautiful, sensual fascinating physique. Her talent blurs the distinction between the ideal and the mistress and male and female. She is everything all together, and appropriate postmodern figure. She achieves dual identity, slave in Hasmukh's point of view while an owner, a democrat in her point own view. The woman like Sonal too is fascinated towards her multidimensional personality. She thinks that Kiran is very lucky and she knew all because she is educated. But yet another truth is revealed in her response to Sonal:

> Kiran: wrong, I learnt my lessons from being so close to life; I learnt my lessons from watching my mother tolerating my father when he came home every day with bottles of rum wrapped in newspapers. As watched him beating her up and calling her names! I learnt what life was when my mother pretended she was happy in front of me and my brothers, so that we wouldn't have my father. And I learnt when I kept my mother away from my father so that in return he would remain silent for those three hours when he came home, and before he fell asleep on the dining table, too drunk to harm us

> anymore. I served him those drinks, waiting for that moment when he would become unconscious and I would say a prayer.... Thank God he was too drunk to impose himself on us! Yes Mrs. Mehta. (*Collected Plays*, 2000: 508)

Her familial back ground, the hidden truth of her life is historically and typically a dehumanizing agency for any raw human being. She was brought up in hatred, in a barbaric environment where no one can dream of morality and humanity, the true-essence of life. The preachers of morals and experts of a cultured society would never agree with that in a bar like home, filled with hatred and terror, a woman like Kiran can succeeds in grooming her personality better and comparatively more skilled than of those who come of sophisticated society. However, it becomes evident that her childhood was deprived of parental love, care and childish spontaneity which is many times more painful than the deprived childhood of Hasmukh who had lost his mother and what is praiseworthy is that she does not regret over her past rather struggles to come out a winning her a powerful personality. Kiran's evolution to such a stature despite limitless unbearable adversities in her life is itself a brilliant example of postmodern realities. She glides forward irrespective of social archetypes set for women.

However, Kiran's disclosure of her familial degenerating patriarchal treatment raises feminist questions how a woman, her mother suffered her entire life in the hands of a drunkard. It reports miserable condition of married women but at the same time Dattani makes his character treat this problem not by politicizing it on feminist perspective but solving it as a rationalist. And the rationale could be achieved only through true education, sincerity and cooperation with a humanist attitude. Kiran, thus, inaugurates postmodern Feminism.

There is no logic in saying her good or bad. The definition of 'good' and 'bad' ideal and 'mean' is perceptional and deconstructional. She defies her father for his drinks and barbarism; she is rude and uncultured for her father but she escapes her mother; for her she is a good daughter. When she exercises the dictates of the Will to teach the lesson to Ajit, his wife Preeti and his mother Sonal, Hasmukh regards her to be a good employee or trustee but when she uses her own mind in identifying Hasmukh's real personality and disclosing it to his wife, he feels irritated. When she claims that making his Will Hasmukh, thought he has won while he is failure a complete failure; for he appears to be a shadow of his own father. He actually exists nowhere rather Ajit is winner; for he defies being the shadow of his father therefore, he does exist and achieves his own identity and personality.

In the play *Where There is a Will* Dattani fuses Shakespeare, Eugene O' Neil and Browning taking ghost to present the past, expressionism to portray hidden reality and dramatic monologue to clarify what goes in the mind of a characters. In Shakespeare's Hamlet, ghost appears to tell the truth that his death was not an accident but a murder plotted by his own brother Claudius and his wife Gertrude. He, then, instigates his son Hamlet to take revenge of his father's assassination, as his true son. But in Dattani's play spirit of Hasmukh appears not to take revenge but to watch the execution of his Will because he is not satisfied with the work efficiency of his son Ajit, daughter-in-law Preeti and his wife Sonal. He has doubts that his son would be a big failure and the company will fall to bankrupt. That is why he wants to teach a lesson to his son, daughter-in-law and wife. But Dattani's purpose here is to show the effects of a post-industrialist society on man. Hasmukh assumes himself a big success in capital letters, a success of power control of a capitalist. The playwright, in Act II, makes him present through his spirit even after his death, and to make him realize how he appears to be a failure; how his power is destabilized by his own trustee Kiran, and how his hierarchical position is democratized. Kiran Jhaberi whom he makes tool of his ruling rod to teach a lesson to his wife Sonal, Son Ajit and daughter-in-law Preeti, develops a co-operative human relation and makes him helpless to realize the misdoings of his dictatorship. Kiran degrades him in communicating with his wife Sonal as:

> Kiran: I should have hated him like I should have hated my father, my brother and my husband. But all I felt for him is pity.
>
> Hasmukh: Enough! I say enough! I paid you to do my work. Not to ridicule me.
>
> Kiran: Even his attempts at ruling over you after his death, through his Will, are pathetic (Hasmukh sticks his finger into his ears and shuts his eyes).
>
> (*Collected Plays*, 2000: 510)

Hasmukh's Will appears as self paradox—the brilliant mode of postmodernism. Linda Hutcheon writes:

> It is part of the postmodernist stand to confront the paradoxes of fictive/historical representation, the particular/the general, and the present/the past. And this confrontation is itself contradictory, for it refuses to recuperate or dissolve either side of the dichotomy, yet it is more than willing to exploit both. (Hutcheon, 1988: 106)

The only reason he wanted to do it is that because his father had ruled over his family. All his life he was merely being a good boy to his father. Disobedience to patriarchal hierarchy and dictatorship and bold spirit of enquiry into all matters dissolving the boundaries of hierarchy, brings every human being on a flat surface where everyone stands on the same level is a postmodernist temper of human society. Kiran Jhaberi appears a representative of democracy where everyone will be free to his/her decision to act on his own will rather than the orders/duties imposed by a Court Will.

Moreover, the technique employed by Dattani to make man soul searching through the fusion of past (the dead man) and future (proceedings of his Will) is a postmodern human tendency. Presentation of the past (dead Hasmukh) with that of his future prospects (his Will) together on the same stage at the same time is typical postmodern scene in an Indian theatre.

Another blend that Dattani employed is of the fusion of Hindu Myth with that of science in post-industrial age. According to Hindu mythology, it is believed that any person, who dies with his/her unfulfilled desire/s, never reaches to heaven, to God's abode. His/her spirit keeps wandering around his wish/es, plan/s and desire/s. However, in the scientific age everything has its logic and based on facts and figures of scientific objectivity, with an evidence of experimentation at any time. In scientific and industrial age one can enlist his future plans and desires through a Will enforceable by the Honourable Court. Dattani, meticulously presents these binaries on the stage at the same time. When Kiran excuties as per the guidelines of the Will, the spirit of Hasmukh finds solace and compliments Kiran for her execution as, "Hasmukh: Bravo! That is what I wanted to hear! (Dances). She has learnt her lesson! (To the audience). Now you can go home and I can go to heaven" (*Collected Plays*, 2000: 50).

Works Cited

Barry, Peter. *Beginning Theory: An Introduction to Literary and Cultural Theories*. Manchester and New York: Manchester University Press, 2002. Print.

Benjamin, Walter. "Theses on the Philosophy of History" in *Illumination*. London: Fontana, 1992. Print.

Butcher, S.H. *The Poetics of Aristotle ed*. London: Macmillan, 1902. Print and E-Book.

Dattani, Mahesh. *Collected Plays*. New Delhi: Penguin Books India Pvt. Ltd, 1994. Print.

——. *Me and My Plays*. New Delhi: Penguin Books India Pvt. Ltd, 2014. Print.

Hutcheon, Linda. *A Poetics of Postmodernism: History, Theory, Fiction*. London & New York: Routledge, 1988. Print.

Levi, Primo. *The Drowned and the Saved*. London: Abacus, 1994. Print.

Lyotard, Jean-Francois. *The Postmodern Explained to Children*. London: Turnaround, 1992. Print.

Shakespeare, William. *Hamlet*. New Delhi: Unique Publishers, 1997. Print.

Walsmley, Chris Snipp. "Postmodernism" in *Literary Theory and Criticism*. Ed. Patricia Waugh. New Delhi: Oxford University Press, 2012. Print.

Waugh, Patricia. *Literary Theory and Criticism*. India: Oxford University Press, 2012. Print.

3

Mahesh Dattani's *Seven Steps around the Fire*: Travails of the Third Sex

Sarika Kanjlia

Even in these contemporary times, when the world has made a global progress in almost all the fields be it technical, academics, sports, science and research, be it politics, or any arena to speak of, there are still many important issues left unaddressed in the Indian context. Besides women related issues, one community that has always got the step motherly treatment from the society is that of Eunuchs (*Hijras*) in India. They have practically no acceptance, no respectable identity and no protection of law. They suffer hugely from prejudice and abuse which often gets translated into violence. The main factor behind this is that society is not able to conform the Eunuchs to the accepted gender divisions. Male and female are the only sexual categories which have secured social approval. Eunuchs, as they do not fit into these two classes, have to bear the brunt of social ostracism and contempt. The community of Eunuchs is marginalized and do not enjoy any social, political and legal rights. The cruel social forces do not permit these underprivileged people to enjoy a respectable status in the society. Mahesh Dattani gives the Eunuchs of India a platform to give a vent to their pent up feelings and emotions through his play *Seven Steps around the Fire* (2005). The case of a member of the community, that is Kamala, is presented in the play who secretly marries the son of a minister and has to bear the death penalty. The innocents of the community get embroiled falsely in the murder case. The patriarchal set up of the society that has made them incapacitated to work has largely been questioned.

The path trudged by human beings has never been very easy. But the human tendency has always been towards its enlightenment and emancipation. The philosophers and creative writers have always engaged themselves in the endeavour to build a healthy and better society by generating the feelings of compassion, love and empathy among the people for the underprivileged sections of the society who have been deprived of the basic rights of happiness and a respectable living. Since ages, man, in order to establish his superiority over those low in rank, caste, race, economic status, religion and so on has exercised authority. In 1980, Gayatri Spivak, wrote of subalterns,

> It denotes to the general attribute of subordination in South Asian Society whether this expressed in terms of caste, class, age, gender and office or any other way. (Gayatri Spivak, *Subaltern Studies*, 1982)

In this regard many movements have been organised from time to time and efforts have been made in order to provide social and psychological freedom to the subalterns. The post-colonial poets and critics specially have made a forceful effort to release the vast majority of people from the oppression and humiliation which they have been suffering since ages.

Mahesh Dattani, the first Indo-English playwright to win the prestigious Sahitya Academy Award, is a dramatist of the modern times who has won considerable repute through his plays on contemporary issues. He has very subtly created a niche in the hearts of his audience by bringing to the fore the emotional pathos of the marginalised and unrecognised sections of the society. He has dealt with many burning issues such as identity crises as in *Tara*, sufferings of AIDS victims as in *Ek Alag Mausam*, about the Homosexuals as in *On a Muggy Night in Mumbai* and so on. The most conspicuous feature of his plays is the wide range of themes that he deals with in his writings. Through his play *Seven Steps around the Fire*, he makes a bold attempt to provide central space to the community of Eunuchs.

He has spotlighted the plight of the *hijras* in the Indian society who are always discarded.

In order to have an in depth knowledge of the play, it is essential to have some basic information about the term *hijra*. The term *hijra*, of course, is of Urdu origin, a combination of Hindi, Persian and Arabic, literally means 'neither male nor female'. Another legend traces their ancestry to the Indian myth from the *Ramayana*. The legend says that once as Lord Rama was going to cross the river and to go on exile in the forest, all the people of the city wanted to follow him. Overwhelmed by their affection, he requested them to turn back by saying, *men and women, turn back*. Some of his male followers did not know what to do. They could not disobey him. But at the same time they did not want to leave him also. So they sacrificed their masculinity, to become neither men nor women, and followed him to the forest. Rama was pleased with their devotion and blessed them.

Tracing their history, they have a record of more than 4,000 years. They sing at the weddings and at childbirth with other *hijras* and people give them money otherwise they put a curse on them. They are considered as the 'chosen of God' and the curse by them cannot be revoked. The word 'Eunuchs' denotes the idea of "a castrated man", especially one in charge of a harem or a high voiced "singer." In ancient India, kings used to keep these Eunuchs for the management of women's chambers. It is evident that *hijra* community in spite of being sexually handicapped, are gifted with identical potential and human sensibility. There are ample evidences in history that kings used to encourage these eunuchs for sexual prostitution. According to social conventions, they are not permitted to live in the respectable society. It is the horror of social convention that they are not even permitted to achieve professional skills to earn their bread and butter. The venues of education are closed for them. Many of them are obliged to die without proper medical care because doctors take it as their misfortune to attend them. The play *Seven Steps around the Fire,* is the first authentic representation of the community of Eunuchs in theatre.

The play *Seven Steps around the Fire* is constructed on the lines of a detective story. The story revolves around the murder case of a eunuch Kamala, who is both young and beautiful. At the very onset, we come across Uma Rao who is the wife of Suresh, the Jail Superintendent. She is doing her research in Sociology and is the daughter of the Vice Chancellor of Bangalore University. Uma resolves to unveil the mystery of Kamala's murder. Instead of any run of the mill type cases of domestic violence and dowry deaths, she takes up the case of Kamala for which one of the members of the community, Anarkali, has been falsely accused. Uma, relegating the topic of her thesis, decides to take up the case of Anarkali, to articulate the mute voices of eunuchs by bringing them to the centre from the margins and expose the community of elitists that drags them to the margins in order to maintain their class superiority. From the dramatic point of view, the script showing the conflict of social commitments and the obligations of interpersonal relationships is very strong. The play *Seven Steps around the Fire* begins with the presence of Uma in the office of the Superintendent of Police. She wants to meet the jail inmates in order to fulfil the conditions of her thesis. There in one of the jails she happens to see Anarkali whose presence there entices her. Eunuchs have genderless identity but Uma addresses Anarkali with the pronoun "she". In contrast to her sympathy, Munuswamy, the assistant of Suresh, pours all contempt against Anarkali by ruthlessly addressing her by using the pronoun 'it'. He asserts, *It will talk to you*. He uses highly abusive tone in talking to her and doesn't consider her to be human at all. Anarkali, being a victim of the class consciousness of elitists, becomes aggressive and non-cooperative towards Uma. She even refuses to meet Uma at first mistaking her for a journalist. The suspended fury bursts out with the sympathy of Uma. Uma with her patience and immense human sympathy subsides Anarkali's anger and wins her confidence. She even assures her release. Confessing her innocence in Kamala's murder case, Anarkali admits, *I didn't kill her. She was my sister*. What makes the plight of hijras more intense is that they are so used to this hatred that it has become a part of their psyche and they have compromised with it. Their interaction with the general society and other individuals does not lead to any kind of happiness. Anarkali scratches the face of Kamala with a knife, because she knows that they can only be treated with hatred in the society and if someone loves a *hijra*, that can just lead to some tragedy. The tragic plight of *hijra* community is evidenced when Anarkali discloses her experience to Uma:

> .... So many times I warned her. First I thought Salim was taking her for his own pleasure. When she told me about Subbu, madam, I tried to stop her. I fought with her. I scratched her face, hoping she will become ugly and Subbu will forget her. He wanted to marry her... I was there at their wedding...she gave me that picture to show to Champa. I saw the men coming for her. I told her to run.... (*Collected Plays II*, 2005: 41)

Dattani strongly believes that the transformation in the attitude of this community of marginalized is possible through love, compassion and understanding. It gives them hope and confidence to realize their own self and to reconstruct the inner strength of will to resist the forces of oppression. The irony is evident in the decision of Suresh who commands that Anarkali should be put in the male prison. On being questioned by Uma, as to why Anarkali has been thus kept, he comments very contemptuously, *They are as strong as horses* and presents whole situation with a wild laughter, "They are all just castrated degenerate men. They fought like dogs every day..." (*Collected Plays II*, 2005: 42). Dattani asserts:

> There are transsexuals all over the world and India is no exception. The purpose of this study is to show their position in society. Perceived as the lowest of the low, they yearn for family and love. (*Collected Plays II*, 2005: 43)

The first and foremost reason for their being treated like this is that they are sexually handicapped and hence different from others biologically. The second and the most important reason for ill treating them is their poverty. The poor in this world are not treated as human beings at all. They are subjected to all types of humiliations, cruelty and contempt and are deprived of their basic right to a decent and respectable life.

The *hijra* community is deprived of several rights because our society recognizes only two sexes and they are the neglected gender. Dattani is probably the first playwright who has written a full length play on them. For the very first time they got the light of the day in the theatre as human beings with an awareness of their self who crave for a respectable space in the society. Remarking on the theme of the play, Dr. Beena Agarwal remarks:

> Dattani in the process of engineering the current of Indian drama by bringing it closer to the real life experiences tried to articulate the voice of the oppressed sections of the society whose identity is shrouded in the cover of myths and social prejudices. They have been dragged in darkness, doomed to survive in perpetual silence bearing the oppressive burden of hegemony of the elitist class. Dattani within the framework of dramatic structure, tries to investigate the identities of those who occupy no space in social order. (Beena Aggarwal, *Mahesh Dattani's Plays: A New Horizon in Indian Theatre,* 2011: 34)

It is a protest play based on the exclusion some sections of the society who do not conform to certain man made parameters of respectable society. Dattani underlines the fact that other than the social customs and bindings, all the members of the marginalised groups, be it the untouchables and coolies of Mulk Raj Anand or the gays, lesbians, or eunuchs of Mahesh Dattani, have a 'self' that longs for dignity and when they are denied the same, they try to free themselves of such customs. When they protest, most of the times their voice is suppressed by those in power. Dattani has added a new dimension to the theatre by taking up such themes in his plays. Bijay Kumar Das remarked:

> Dattani has done a good job by introducing a new theme to Indian English drama. Conservatives and social activists should not turn a blind eye to reality.... We have to accept the reality of life, however, painful that might be. (Bijay Kumar Das, *Form and Meaning in Mahesh Dattani's Plays,* 2008: 17)

It is probably one of the best plays of Dattani that discusses the socio-psychological crisis of the *hijras* who are torn between the social customs and their personal desires. On being shown sister like affinity by Uma, Anarkali becomes emotional and is ready to divulge her conditions of life, "If you were a hijra, I would have made you my sister". She expresses her doubts, "They will kill me also if I tell the truth. If I don't tell the truth, I will die in jail". This dramatizes their sense of helplessness, anguish, insecurities, fears and frustration of living in such type of social set up. For Anarkali, the love and compassion of Uma brings a new ray of hope and she tells her their neglected dwelling place. In her quest to clear many doubts regarding the *hijras* and their social positioning, Uma resolves to go to Shivajinagar as told by Anarkali in order to meet Champa, their head and care taker. When she comes to Champa, she is found enjoying the company of members of her community. As Uma tries to involve her in conversation regarding Kamala and Anarkali, she bursts out thus, "We cannot speak...when we want to speak nobody listens when we cannot speak" (*Collected Plays I*, 2005: 53). She further says, "There is no world for a hijra other than the one we make for ourselves" (*Collected Plays I,* 2005: 53). With pain and anguish she says, "You don't know how much we all loved her! You will not understand. I loved her more than you can love your daughter! You don't know". These statements of Champa clearly show that despite the fact that they are marginalised, they also possess a loving and caring heart, a characteristic feature of a normal human being. Uma (thought):

> Nobody seems to know anything about them. Neither do they. Did they come to this country with Islam, or are they a part of our glorious Hindu tradition? Why are they so obsessed with weddings and ceremonies of childbirth? How do they come to know of these weddings? Why do they just show up without being invited? Are they just extortionists? And why do they not take singing lessons? (*Collected Plays II,* 2005: 16-17)

Uma realises that Champa is the only person who can bail Anarkali out because nobody else would care. She borrows Fifty Thousand rupees from her father and gives it to Champa for Anarkali's release. Champa's abode reveals to Uma the remoteness and invisibility of the *hijras* from the social stream. Those who try to take a breath of freedom have to face consequences. The same thing happened with Kamala, who loved Subbu and secretly married him, but was eventually burnt to death on the bidding of Mr. Sharma, who is an influential politician and Subbu's father.

Dattani makes a bold attempt to give central space in the mainstream drama to the community of Eunuchs in this play. The cruel society denies family bliss to the eunuchs but ironically their presence is essential on the occasions of marriage and child birth. Uma's whole endeavour is directed to expose the double standards and corruption of ruling class. At Champa's place, Uma comes to know about some secret involvement of Salim, Mr. Sharma's servant, in Kamala murder case. She visits Sharma's place to identify the identity of Salim and his involvement in the case. When Uma arrives at Mr. Sharma's place, she finds his son, Subbu there. Mr. Sharma, the minister, tries to prevent Subbu from getting involved in the case. Dattani here presents highly emotional situations to make the presentation effective. In the later part of the play events like the sudden release of Anarkali, the marriage of Subbu to a girl who is socially acceptable, the appearance of Champa with her trail on the occasion of marriage of Subbu and the nervousness of Suresh prepare very strong dramatic situations to investigate those terrains of human consciousness where social dualities come to an end. Mr. Sharma is more agitated to see Champa, as he is insecure of his reputation and of getting caught in the murder case. As soon as the dance of Champa begins, in the image of dancing Anarkali, the image of dead Kamala starts haunting Subbu's mind. As a result, Subbu loses control over himself and declares, "You can't keep me away from Kamala". To take the best of Subbu's nervousness, Champa takes the photograph and gives it to him. As soon as he looks at the photograph, the living paraphernalia suspends and he starts identifying Kamala with Anarkali. In this state of masochism, Subbu reveals the secret of his relationship with Kamala and also the secret of the murder of Kamala. In depression, Subbu takes the gun from Suresh,

Uma's husband and kills himself. It is only after the death of Subbu that Kamala's murder mystery is resolved. Even Subbu in the name of the power of his father fails to retain his voice and status. Dattani in his representation of Eunuchs seems to agree that the marginalized can't raise their voice against humiliation and injustice. Subbu dies but both Suresh and Mr. Sharma were not ready to listen to the voice of Anarkali. They are not even ready to consider the happiness of their family members. Uma concludes:

> They have no voice. The case was hushed up and it was not even reported in the newspaper.... Subbu's suicide was written off as an accident. The photograph was destroyed. So are the lives of two young people...but Anarkali's blessings remain with me.... I did not want her blessings for a child. All I want is what they want...to move on, to love to love. (*Collected Plays II*, 2005: 61)

The arguments enunciated in the present critical interpretation evince that in case of marginalized communities, the psychic subjugation has far reaching consequences. The awareness about the suffering of the marginalized communities is a realization of the perceptions of life that can ensure better understanding of human relationship. Champa's quest to love and to live is a call from margin to seek a respectable space in the centre. Dattani organizes the events in the play to establish that the innate natural deficiency should not be exploited as the mechanism of subjugation. The unbridled passion for happiness and personal relationship of Champa and Anarkali suggests that eunuchs are not marginalized by nature and God but they are marginalized by the system which does not ensure an equitable distribution of wealth. The contribution of Dattani is his positive vision that the involvement in personal relationship can be taken as a safe panacea for the redemption of the suffering of marginalized communities. The idea of associating the social curse with personal relationship gives an intense dramatic quality and assigns a new direction to subaltern studies.

Uma-Suresh relationship gives another dimension to the plot of the play. While Uma is passionate, caring and loving, her husband Suresh is highly practical. He knows the influence of the people like Mr. Sharma who is a politician and is on duty to protect him and check the security on Subbu's marriage. He knows that Anarkali is innocent but uses her as somebody has to be shown as a culprit. He is more interested in pleasing his seniors as he is very much worried about his promotion. While Uma works selflessly to provide justice to the victims, Suresh is out to protect them from public disgrace. He is shown to be quite callous in his attitude towards other human beings especially those low in rank. He argues with Uma regarding her request to have a test of his sperm count as this hurts his male ego. This clearly shows the hypocritical attitude of a typical male who publicly sneers at the eunuchs for their sexual handicap whereas he himself is no better than them. The thing that gives them an edge over eunuchs is the rich class to which they belong. Jeremy Mortimer says:

> Mahesh Dattani does not seek to cut a path through the difficulties, his characters encounter, instead he leads his audience to see just how caught up we all are in the complications and contradictions of our values and assumptions. And by revealing the complexity, he makes the world a richer place for all of us. (Jeremy Mortimer. quoted from *The Hindu*: Sunday, August 7, 2005. *Literary Review*. "Unmasking Our Worlds", 3)

To conclude, we can say that Mahesh Dattani's play *Seven Steps around the Fire* is a play par excellence. It brings to the surface the cruelty, humiliation, hypocrisy, denial of basic rights to the common underprivileged people of the society, be it the untouchables, the workers, or the eunuchs perpetrated by the rich and the powerful. The *hijra* community because of their poverty faces the disgust and dislike of the people. Their natural handicap becomes secondary in the wake of the class based society of ours. Had they been rich and influential, things would have been different. But now they are considered the lowest of the low on the rungs of social ladder. They face a double jeopardy as they are the victims of nature as well as of the society. The bias that they have to suffer does not allow them to lead a normal life. They are not even recognised as the members of the society. Their helplessness, fears and frustrations are highlighted in the play. They are human beings with no voice, no right to develop relationships, no love, no justice and probably no hope of acceptability in the society.

References

Aggarwal, Beena. *Mahesh Dattani's Plays: A New Horizon in Indian Theatre*. Jaipur: Book Enclave, 2011: 34. Print.

Das, Bijay Kumar. *Form and Meaning in Mahesh Dattani's Plays*. New Delhi: Atlantic Publishers, 2008: 17. Print.

Dattani, Mahesh. *Collected Plays II*. New Delhi: Penguin, 2005. Print.

Gandhi, Leela. *Post Colonial Theory: A Critical Introduction*. Delhi: Oxford University Press, 1999. Print.

Mortimer, Jeremy, BBC. *Literary Review*. "Unmasking Our Worlds", Quoted from *The Hindu*: Sunday, August 7, 2005, p. 3. Print.

Spivak, Gayatri. *Subaltern Studies*. (ed.) R. Guha, Vol. I. Delhi: Oxford University Press, 1982. Print.

4

Incest: Cause of Pain and the Rift between Mother and Daughter

Mamta Khosla

Mahesh Dattani is a leading professional playwright for whom theatre is an art with function. He believes that:

> Theatre survives only when we see our aspirations, our struggles, our hopes and values reflected in it and when we don't see ourselves in the theatre, we'll see stop believing in theatre.... Theatre is a reflection of what you observe, to do anything more would be to become didactic and then it ceases to be theatre. (Prasad, 2007: 262)

It is seen that unlike other Indian English writers who lays emphasis on history, myths and scriptures—Dattani concentrates on contemporary society and reality in the fast changing world. From his years of being a "reluctant" playwright to a highly successful (and celebrated) one, Dattani has carried on the business, as he says, "of holding a mirror up to society" (Dattani, 2000: xv) through an art that is both entertaining as well as issue-based, self aware and rooted in its milieu.

It can be said that Dattani's contribution to Indian English Drama lies in bringing everyday problems in contemporary society and taboo subjects into the realms of drama. He himself says:

> I write for my milieu, for my time and place middle-class and urban Indian.... My dramatic tensions arise

> from people who aspire to freedom from society.... I am not looking for something sensational, which audiences have never seen before...some subjects, which are under-explored, deserve their space. It's no use brushing them under the carpet. We have to understand the marginalized, including the gays. Each of us has a sense of isolation within given contexts. That's what makes us individual. (Quoted from *The Hindu*: Out of the Closet, on the Screen. March 9, 2003, Sunday)

Reading his plays his words can be seen as been truly implemented. That is to say issue like homosexuality, gender discrimination, communalism and the child sexual abuse, etc. find an honest and candid delineation in his plays. Basically all this shows that his plays focus on many contemporary social issues and because of his contemporaneity his personality cannot be easily sidelined. In other words, his dramatic guts and artistic perceptions are a part of his individuality that make his position unique in literature.

He uses the world of comic theatre to encase the bitterness of the truths he is dealing with. After reading his plays one can say that his plays are meant to be performed, not just read as literature. He needed English plays to perform and they were unavailable. So he wrote them not as a writer writing a self-consciously 'literary' work but as a performer amalgamating the 'extra-literary' polyphony of the stage in his writing and keeping audience reception in his mind. That has perhaps made all the difference to the manner in which Dattani has managed so fluently to communicate with such audiences, as well as the reason, ultimately, for the 'literary' quality of his output.

The most characteristic quality of Dattani's plays is the wide range of themes that he deals in his writing. His themes speak volumes about the social taboos that we see in our society. Some of his plays are eloquent defenses of society's outcasts and would be rebels, people forced to live double lives in order to satisfy the prying eyes of society. To say, Mahesh Dattani's plays often feature characters who are questioning their identity which feel isolated in some way. In other words, his characters are a metaphor for the unspoken and unexpressed within all of us. Moreover, he gives expression to the longing and aspirations of the middle class Indians. As John McRae puts it, "Dattani is the voice of India now".

His achievement as a playwright depends on the fact that his plays are a slice of life. They present reality as it exists. He writes about what he observes and an excellent example of his observation is the play *Thirty Days in September*. Dattani wrote this play after being approached by the NGO-Rahi (Recovery and healing of Incest) who counsel survivors of childhood sexual abuse. When they approached Dattani to write, on the subject he immediately said yes. And with great zeal and insight through this play he explores a dark area in our social and family life.

This play reminds us of a changing society under the impact of globalization where morality is thrown into the wind. Before writing this play he met seven or eight adult women who spoke to him about their childhood experiences where they were sexually abused by their own family members. Learning about their experiences from them and using his own imagination in *Thirty Days in September* he shows the impact of sexual abuse on the psyche of the abused child. Undoubtedly, it is a dark and gripping tale about crisis that goes unspoken in many communities that is sexual abuse of children. The play begins with Mala talking to an imagined counselor which brings the dilemma in her mind to light. She frankly reveals her real name, Mala Khatri and confidently asserts that it is the person, who molested her, should hide herself from being recognized because she has not been a participant but a victim of his beastly passion. On the other hand in her taped voice she says:

> ...don't know how to begin.... Today is the 30th of September 2001 and my name is... I don't think I want to say my name. I am sorry. I know it is all my fault really.... It must be. I must have asked for it. It's not anybody's fault, except my own. Sometimes I wish that my mother.... (*Collected Plays II*, 2005: 9)

On the contrary, these words of Mala present her as a more confused and to a great extent, a nervous person. She assumes herself responsible for the havoc which turned her attitude to life and at the other time she suspects her mother to be behind her destruction.

These counseling sessions and Mala's taped conversation have continuously been used by Dattani as a means of self-revelation. Through them the conflict between Mala's conscious and unconscious mind is revealed. Listening to these conservations of Mala the reader can say that the play is based on the torment of Mala, the protagonist who lives with the haunting memories of her abused past. As one reads the play one finds she was exploited physically by her maternal uncle in their infancy. Her uncle, Vinay is portrayed like an evil spell that casts its shadow of doom throughout her life. In other words, throughout the play we see that her abuser-her uncle sub-consciously lives with her all the time, as part of her daily reflections and as a result even her natural growth is damaged. Because of this she is not able to have any relationship with any male beyond an ominous thirty day period. She could not stay with any male beyond this time because her tormentor would never allow her to do so. Because of all this she became free with young men.

In the course of the play she tries again and again to tell her mother about the travails she has been suffering but her mother always ignored her pleas by calling them dreams. We as a reader see that instead of assuaging her agony, Shanta sought shelter in the lap of Lord Krishna all the while seeking consolation in the song—*Mere to Girdhar Gopal, doosro no koi, Mere to Girdhar Gopal.* She always preferred escapism to fulfilling her daughter's emotional expectation of giving her strength. We as a reader see that whenever the daughter came out with her woes in front of her mother, she pretended it to be something less important and never responded positively to strengthen her emotionally. On the contrary, she immediately took to feeding her with her favourite *allu parathas* as this gave her (Mala) a temporary relief as she started feeling that that was the cure for her restless heart, hurt and her crying. But in reality it was her mother's way to pacify.

Shanta was very much aware of the terrible reality that her daughter was suffering from and as she was unable to help so every time she rushes to seek help from Lord Krishna. Mala detains her from taking shelter in the image of God. She says:

> I cannot believe. I simply cannot believe that.... Do you really think that is what I am talking about? Ask yourself honestly. Tell me. No don't look at your God, look at me, look me in the eye and tell me-yes, that is all that you are talking about. (*Collected Plays II*, 2005: 25)

Her words show that she not only bears the pain of sexual assault in her childhood but also equally suffers the emotional hurt caused by her mother's silence against her molestation which subsists in her unconscious mind. This silence of her mother tears her apart and at the same time it increases her rage. She is not able to accept her mother's stoicism. She cannot bear her mother's silence and negligence. She hates her mother's attitude of rushing to take support from Lord Krishna during most of her critical moments.

As she grows her traumatic experience of physical exploitation and her mother's indifferent attitude towards it starts coming at the surface level resulting in a lifelong clash between mother and daughter. Besides this we can see Mala also bears a grudge against the male-dominated society and thus when Deepak proposes to her she becomes shocked and amazed and because of this she turns down Deepak's proposal of marriage. It can be said Mala's reaction comes out of her anger caused by her mother's inaction to protect her from her uncle. Mala gives two reasons for her fall: the first, the Western values which extol permissiveness and the second, her mother's inability to control her. She says:

> I don't know why. I just don't understand.... Please don't ask me why I do it. It's just a game.... What I am doing is terribly wrong! But.... I like it. I suppose it's these Western values, I wish I were more traditional then I wouldn't behave like this.... The only person who can, who could have prevented all this is my mother. (*Collected Plays II*, 2005: 18)

Her confessing and confused tone to the counselor throws some light on her 'inner space' arena. She conveys him her inner turmoil and tells him the reason of her behaving in such a way is beyond her imagination. She considers herself to be a bad and characterless person. She is afraid that she has imbibed in all the Western values and would prefer to be traditional. And finally she tells the counselor that her mother could have warned her to stop all this.

The play shows that Mala is not interested in marriage but wants to mix with many a men to gratify her desire. She goes to a party and dances with a man (Ravi) who came with his fiance, Radhika. Moreover, she encourages the man to take liberty with her and most shockingly Mala tells him, "Do whatever you want with me, but take me with you now" (*Collected Play II*, 2005: 21).

One can notice Mala analyses all the events that have taken place in her life and the repercussions that have followed it and because of this she is filled with self-hatred and she herself considers herself a loose woman. In Act II, Mala reveals that she has slept with many a men—not just the men in the office but his uncle and cousin as well. Slowly her anger is diverted towards her mother, she suffers the emotional hurt caused by her mother's silence against her molestation which fills her consciousness.

Dattani reveals layer after layer of Mala's traumatized psyche. She is guilt ridden and holds her mother as well as herself responsible for her physical and mental disorder. Interrogating her she asks her:

> Where were you when he locked the door to your bedroom while I was napping in there? Where were you during those fifteen minutes when he was destroying my soul? Fifteen every day of my summer holidays, add them up. Fifteen minutes multiplied by thirty or thirty-one or whatever. That's how long or how little it took for you to send me to hell for the rest of my life! Surely you must have known, Ma. (*Collected Plays II*, 2005: 53)

Sexually molested by her maternal uncle, Mala faces betrayal at the hands of her mother. Portraying the relationship between mother and daughter, Dattani has tried to shed light on the fact that betrayal in any close relationship, as Mala realizes, is as painful as sexual abuse. In his conversation with Lakshmi Subramanyam, Dattani says:

> Though sexual abuse is at the core of my play, the mother-daughter relationship is equally important. The main protagonist, who has suffered at the hands of her uncle, feels a deep sense of betrayal that her mother did not stop the abuse and failed in her role as protector. (133)

Mala even goes to the extent of saying that it was because of getting financial assistance that her mother remained silent. She cries out, *He bought your silence. So that you can never tell anyone what he did to your daughter!* His words show that along with humiliation of her body, her spirit, her privacy and her innocence is also raped. Thus, Mala's anguish and pain is intensified from her realization of her mother's betrayal. In this regard, Asha Kuthari Chaudhuri observes, Child sexual abuse spans a range of problems, but it is this complicity of the family through silence and a lack of protest that is the ultimate betrayal for the abused (73).

Further Mala also holds her mother responsible for her father leaving them. She says:

> All night long I had to listen to your mumbling saying you didn't want him near you. You didn't want him touching you. You even moved that horrible picture of your god into my room saying he will protect us. He left because of you. You didn't love him. The only reason you shared my room was because you didn't want to sleep with him...he said to me 'I married a frozen woman.' *A Frozen woman.* (*Collected Plays II*, 2005: 35-36)

These words of Mala hits Shanta hard. Moved by Mala's pain, Shanta reveals the reality of her life and the reason for her keeping her lips shut. She tells how the same man (her brother) exploited her physically and psychologically when she was six and continued it for ten years. Shanta was full of remorse when she recalls the physical exploitation in the past and the subconscious mind makes her feel guilty about it. She confesses before her daughter in the following words:

> I was six, Mala I was six. And he (her brother) was thirteen...and it wasn't only summer holidays. For ten years!...(pointing to the picture of god) I looked to Him.... I lost myself in Him. He helped me. By taking away all feeling. No pain, no pleasure, only silence. Silence means Shanti. Shanti. But my tongue is cut off. No. No. It just fell off somewhere. I didn't use it, no. I cannot shout for help, I cannot say words of comfort, I cannot even speak about it. (*Collected Plays II*, 2005: 55)

Her words show that her tongue was cut down and had fallen down. Thus, when she could not save herself how could she save Mala. Further we can say that her agony could melt stones if stones could be melted and her guilt conscience haunts her without end. Looking at the case of both Mala and Shanta we can say that the play shows exploitation of women by men. In a patriarchal society women become toys at the hands of man. It is social and cultural construct of feminine mind which fights shy of going against men. We can see the agony in Mala's life grew because of Shanta's silence but she was helpless as she too was a victim of incest.

After her mother's revelation Mala realizes that both of them shared the same fate. Their molestation spoilt their lives. They also show typical male-chauvinistic morality in India where women are seen as objects of sexual gratification. In the play, Vinay instead of feeling sorry for what he has been doing very arrogantly says—*You like it! You enjoy it. After four years you have become a whore! At thirteen you are a whore!* He has no feeling of remorse or sympathy for Shanta and Mala who undergo mental and physical sufferings. He does not feel shame when he is called 'Bhaia' by Shanta, instead he confidently claims to act like a father figure when Mala's marriage is concerned. Moreover, he who ruins Mala in her teens does not hesitate in using the expression *She is like my daughter*. It can be said that showcasing all this Dattani has mocked at the traditional concept of relationship which explains the purity of the relationship between brother and sister and warns the society of being cautious of relatives like Vinay.

Her mother's revealation of the fact that she also suffered the molestation for ten years by the same person when she was six, moves Mala and she regrets:

> While I accused you of not recognising my pain, you never felt any anger at me for not recognizing yours. We were both struggling to survive but—I never acknowledged your struggle. (*Collected Plays II,* 2005: 58)

In a conversation with Anitha Santhanam, Mahesh Dattani remarks:

> It's the silence and the betrayal of the family that affects me the most. Like in this case, the mother knew that her daughter was being sexually abused by her uncle, but still chose to keep quiet. It's the silence that makes the abused feel betrayed. (Santhanam, 2001)

In this way, both mother and daughter share the same fate. Mala feels guilty of psychologically torturing her mother and begs her forgiveness. She says, *it's not your fauly mother. Just as it it wasn't my fault. Please tell me that.... I know you till, mother. I know you have* (Collected Plays II, 2005: 58).

Thus, the sexual molestation affects both of the victims differently as one is dragooned into bearing it silently due to social pressure and taboos and the other revolts against it. In other words, where Shanta bears the pain in silence, Mala a girl with modern sensibility keeps speaking out against the outrage and revolt against her mother's silence.

It can be said Dattani does not provide readymade solutions or fully resolved ending. He presents the flaw before the people to make them believe that such issues are very much a part of the educated urban society but the people do not want to confront them. He wants to make the people aware of this fact that they are a reality and not just the fantasies of a playwright. He does not punish Vinay. Instead the play ends with the union between mother and daughter which shows that love and care of your family can heal anything. Thus the play shows that though incest threatens to break family, love helps to keep it intact. The union between mother and daughter in the end shows the triumph of love over depression and disintegration of family.

On the whole the play that begins with Mala self-accusation and sense of betrayal towards her mother ends on a happy note with a reunion between mother and daughter in their common emotions of grief and remorse.

Works Cited

Agrawal, Beena. *Mahesh Dattani's Plays: A New Horizon in Indian Theatre*. Jaipur: Book Enclave, 2008. Print.

Chaudhuri, Asha Kuthari. *Contemporary Indian Writers in English*. New Delhi: Cambridge University Press India Pvt Ltd, 2005. Print.

Das, Bijay Kumar. *Form and Meaning in Mahesh Dattani's Plays*. New Delhi: Atlantic Publishers and Distributors (P) Ltd, 2008. Print.

Dattani, Mahesh. *Collected Plays*, Vol. II. New Delhi: Penguin, 2005. Print.

——. Interview by Anitha Santhanam. *'It's the silence that affects me most'*. 2001. Web.

Dhawan, R.K. and Tanu Pant. *The Plays of Mahesh Dattani: A Critical Response*. New Delhi: Prestige Books, 2005. Print.

Joshipura, Pranav. *A Critical Study of Mahesh Dattani's Plays*. New Delhi: Sarup Book Publishers Pvt. Ltd, 2009. Print.

Multani, Angelie. Introduction. *Mahesh Dattani's Plays: Critical Perspectives*. New Delhi: Pencraft International, 2007. Print.

Nagori, S.R. Emotionally Strangulated Relationships in Dattani's *Thirty Days in September*. 2012. Web. 15 May 2013.

Prasad, Amar Nath. *The Dramatic World of Mahesh Dattani: A Critical Exploration*. New Delhi: Sarup Book Publishers Pvt. Ltd, 2009. Print.

——. *The Plays of Mahesh Dattani: A Fine Fusion of Feeling and Form*. New Delhi: Sarup Book Publishers Pvt. Ltd, 2007. Print.

Subramanyam, Lakshmi. *A Dialogue with Mahesh Dattani. Muffled Voices: Women in Modern Indian Theatre*. Ed. New Delhi: Shakti Books, 2002. Print.

5

Identity through the Trajectory of Trust and Distrust: Viewing Muslim Minority in the Modern Secular Framework through *Final Solutions*

Bhaskar Lama

> Can we shake off our prejudices or are they in our psyche like our genes? Will we ever be free or ever-locked in combat.... Arab against Jews, white against blacks, Hindus against Muslims? Are they any final solutions? (Padamsee, 161)

Religion as a category is not a trans-historical phenomenon. It is always defined within social and historical contexts, and even people have specific reasons for defining it in one way or the other. It is out of question to imagine that religion exists in an 'abstract' sense. It can rather be defined in the ontological sense of it being experienced, and operating within the institutions through movements and discussions. It is so because when religion is associated with social and historical contexts then the facts automatically enter into legal dimensions, domestic dimensions and political dimensions. Given the background of religious existence, the vital question to encounter is, "Is it possible to maintain religious tolerance and co-existence within multi-cultural structure?" Moreover, it raises hackles when the question is about the religious tension and sustenance within the modern democratic configuration where secularism is supposed to be the existing order. Within a secular framework, there are more bones of contention with regard to the matters concerning "public versus private", "majority versus minority", "us versus them". In a similar vein we can question the operation of secularism itself, interrogating its sanctity and its functioning. Dattani's play *Final Solutions* (1991), written in the post-colonial era does enable us to view the present Indian scenario (post-partition) under various limelights—secular, modern, communal and religious. The play is an effort to build up the trajectory of the religious community after independence; encoding and decoding all trusts and distrusts between each other.

Final Solutions is the written 'signifier' of the post-partition/ independent India which 'signifies' the progressive history within it. The history is mainly of the turbulent situation which ensued as a result of religious strife. Ineluctably the adverse situation is also fostered by other determiners—economic, political and social. The fact is that partition was based on the ground of securing rights (Muslims wanted to have their rights secured as a Minority group). However, the outline of this division between "religious communities" can be traced to colonial times:

> The division of the Indian population into religious communities was an aspect of colonial thought from the beginning. When the British sought to apply indigenous law, they made a clear-cut division between 'Hindu' and 'Muhammedan' law. The conceptual division was further institutionalised in the census operations, which established a Hindu 'majority' and a Muslim 'minority' that in turn became the basis of electoral, representative politics. (Veer, 11)

During the partition there were Muslims who did not want to move to Pakistan and preferred to stay back in India and the case was same with many Hindus in Pakistan. The imperative question today is in connection with their predicament. Do they live like any other citizen (for e.g. Hindus), with rights? They are counted as a minority. The status of the minority in secularism can always be questioned. One can hardly negate the stereotypical way of looking at them. The major query remains, "How is their identity constructed?" Some of these vital questions are broached by Dattani in *Final Solutions*.

It is quite significant to ascertain the relevance of the concept of secularism and its inception in the Indian context. It is so because of the existing diverse institutions which amalgamate to build the structure and nature of the country. Some of these institutions are religious, economic, political, geographical, and historical. Chatterjee writes that the term "secularism" has very "different meanings" from its "standard" use in the English Language in the Indian terrain (1997, 232). This is mainly due to the prevalence of the two "dissimilar cultures" (the Oriental and the Occidental) which somehow dissembles the equation of similar connotations. However, it would be quite incongruous to concede that the Indian meaning of secularism emerged in "ignorance" of the European or American meanings. There does not exist in any Indian language a term for "secular" or "secularism" which is "standardly used in talking about the role of religion in the modern state and society" (233). The Indian "neologism" for secularism such as *dharma-nirpeksatas*, after translation, somehow connotes the relation between religion and the state. The purpose of injecting secularism upon "deeply religious societies" has been for a "variety of reasons—regulating inter-religious tensions for instance" (Chandhoke, 81). However, I believe that despite the best efforts of secularism, the rebellious religious groups motivated by political ends somehow or the other pose a challenge for its very existence. Therefore, the position of the (religious) minority is always vulnerable and at stake.

It is evident from the above discussion that the diverse cultural dimensions of India do not provide resilience to the equal meaning of the word "secular", as in the West. Talal Asad says that "secularism implies certain reflections of separation between state and religion" (181). He also says that secularism as a political doctrine is closely connected to the formation of religion. It is in a secular state where it becomes essential for the state law to define genuine religion and its boundary. Hence, the term secularism ideally does not offer a simple solution to the divergent context and meaning that it entails. Secularism has been "historically devised to regulate relationships" between people and groups who belong to different and rival "religious persuasions" (Chandhoke, 88). The play *Final Solutions* has a different take with regard to the trajectory that Indian religious history has been building since many years. Despite thriving in the womb of a constitutionally granted 'Secular' and 'Democratic' nation, minorities (religious particularly) have always been under a constant threat. There have always been problems with regard to the temple-mosque controversies which have pepped up unsettling situations across the country. A common "fallacy" is that these passions are "natural" and that the violent struggle is an explosion of pent-up feelings (Veer, 7). The very essence of naturalness can be put under scrutiny when it is culturally influenced and established through everyday performative acts.

Dattani's use of multi-level stagecraft skilfully enables him to capture the historical time sequence within one play. There is a constant to and fro movement in the time sequence. Right from the pre-partition religious uprisings, reflected through Hardika/Daksh to the street riot and the breaking of the idol where the play presently connects. Dattani meticulously connects the wide space and time-frame. There is a subtle endeavour on Dattani's part to recheck the historiography through the limelight of conscience. There is an attempt to juxtapose situation seen from the *a priori*, prejudiced and internalized point of view and later an attempt to rectify it by unravelling the "neutral" standpoint. In other words, if we are given to understand the situation through the myopic perception of the characters, later there is also an attempt to subvert such limited perception by a more unbiased or secular opinion of their guilty conscience. This is perceptible through the change in the nature and mind-set of the characters, from insensitive in the beginning of the play to a more mellow and unprejudiced towards the end.

The whole play is presented as if it were viewed through the eyes of Hardika, the grandmother in the Gandhi family. Hardika can also be considered as a type of chorus because it is through her jottings in her diary and through her "reflections and reactions that the narrative progresses" (Prasad, 84). Through his "unique" device, Dattani presents the teenaged *avatar* of Hardika named Daksha who is simultaneously present on the stage to inform us of the situation five decades back. The play opens with Daksha's first essay in the diary-writing, thereby divulging woman's sensibility to the audience. Incidentally, a major question is about the liminal space that a woman wields, and therefore, her capability to encapsulate issues through her forcefully granted "limited" understanding. It is also about her limitations as a woman in a patriarchal society; her prejudices brewing because of the restrictions imposed on her and at the same time her internalization of the patriarchal notions. Her identity is constructed based on her exclusion: "From the beginning the liberal public sphere excluded certain kinds of people: women, subjects without property, and members of religious minorities" (Asad, 183). Most of the time woman/Daksha's identity is obliterated and it remains within the "mask", like that of the chorus in the play.

In *Final Solutions*, we can find multiple levels of the masks as Dattani's stagecraft itself. Mask could be representing the identity that one puts on as required. It can be seen as make-believe that humans adopt as per the situational demand. The literal change of masks by the mob can be discerned in allegorical terms too. There are times when people take double stance depending upon the situation and this they can do only by putting on the mask of hypocrisy. Mask is also used to cover up many facts and "[at] a more dynamic moments, he [chorus] can use it as a weapon in a stylized fashion" (165). As the Mob/Chorus do not belong to any religion they "ideally should" wear black. Nevertheless, as there is no freedom from the religious context, particularly in a culturally diverse country like India, the "apolitical" stance on religion itself becomes a nihilistic idea. Therefore, the only reality of the Mob/Chorus is the "mask".

Dattani underscores the clash between the fanaticisms of Hindus pitted against that of Muslims. Lack of accommodation between the two communities and unacceptability give rise to acrimony resulting in terrorism and anarchy. The play itself is a question mark on this "age-old enmity" between the two communities wondering for if there would ever be a *Final Solution* to this "endemic" problem (Das, 55). In common parlance, the accusation could also be ascribed to other factors for bringing about the clash and the primary one could be politics. However, as Veer opines:

> Nor is it simply a political trick conjured up by leaders for their own benefit. Such arguments simply overlook the importance of religious meaning and practice in the construction of identity. (7)

Religion has been the cultural essence among Indians, and the determining factors of the society—economic, political and social—are aware about it. It is through the credence of this awareness that they wield expediency to somehow facilitate their own cause, even at the cost of creating a parochial and sectarian environment. In *Final Solutions*, Smita says that they (political parties) hire him (Javed) and many more in the city to "create riots" (195). The people in power are able to hoodwink people by fabricating a discourse of an untoward happening by demonizing the "other" and injecting prejudiced doctrines. In this way, the young minds are swayed in the emotional turmoil of religion and creed, region and language.

From the above-mentioned point, we can generally deduce that it is basically the mark of "exclusion" and "inclusion" that also supplements identity formation. Exclusion inevitably brings in the question of stereotyping and rarefying the "other" where the latter also internalizes this notion. In other words, formation of identity/subjectivity is a dual process where the individual wields his/her limited agency to corroborate the identity conferred on him/her by "hailing" or through "interpellation". Accordingly, the "self" and the "other" take their own "subject-positions". As in the Indian religious context Amin writes: "The sense of belonging—belonging to the present nation—involves the creation and replication of a sense of 'them' and 'us' through icons, stories, and narratives" (2). The "icons, stories, and narratives" would enact as discursive practices to construct the identity of the "other" as would be of the "self."

In the play, there is a stark revelation of the entrenched hypocrisy among individuals. When Ramnik, the liberal-minded fellow blatantly accuses Javed on his prejudiced understanding: How dare you blame your violence on other people? It is in you! You have violence in your mind. Your life is based on violence. Your faith is based... "stops, but it is too late" (198).

We understand that even he is not free from the hands of the prejudice discourse and had been thoroughly putting on the "mask" of being secular and liberal-minded. The representational "mask" which the chorus was putting on, at that specific time, could be metaphorically perceived on Ramnik's face. The exterior self gets splintered from the interior one. After that when the interior comes on the surface we get a new face which is altogether different from what the person's poses.

Alyque Padamsee says, directing *Final Solutions* in Mumbai,

> As I see it, this is a play about transferred resentments. About looking for a scapegoat to hit out when we feel let down, humiliated. Taking out your anger on your wife, children or servants is an old Indian custom...this is, above all, a play about a family with its simmering undercurrents.... (2000, 161)

The question is also about ascertaining the differences in opinion within family members. In doing so it becomes feasible to see the functioning of the (secular) mindset within the familial unit or in the private sphere. Secularism is caught with the fear of "religious intrusion into private life" and Asad gives the reason thus: "...it may be explained by the doctrine that while secular law permits the essential self to make and defend itself, religious prescriptions only confine and dominate it" (186).

We can sense this in the play when we scrutinize the behaviour of different members of the Gandhi family. Javed and Babban, the two Muslim boys take refuge in Ramnik Lal's house while they escape the Hindu mob that was attacking them. Ramnik Gandhi perceives that the boys were victimized by religious fanatics and takes up the onus to save them, "I have to protect them! I need to protect them" (182). He refuses to "throw them out" to the mob even at the cost of his life, "there is nothing you can take from here without killing me first" (182). We locate in him the benevolent sensitivity to stand for someone who is victimized, even at a risk of inviting himself as a "traitor" or "a family of traitors".

On the other hand, we have Ramnik's wife Aruna who is orthodox Hindu and is strictly against the Muslim boys taking refuge in the house. She also wants to drive the boys off because of the fear of being labelled "traitor" and getting victimized, "they'll kill us too" (182)! She does not see any sense in helping people who are of different religions, and moreover, Muslims, against whom there is an ingrained prejudice. She reluctantly offers them water and after the boys drink water, "she holds the glasses with her thumbs and index fingers, on the sides which have not been touched by their lips. Then she takes them away and keeps them separate from the other glasses..." (185). The feeling of disaffection is very much palpable in her action. This is mainly because of the internalization of the religious doctrine which makes it unviable for her to be flexible towards other religions or to be 'secular' either. Then we have Hardika, Ramnik's mother, who is already suffused with lifelong inveterate prejudice, "They killed his grandfather" (179)! She highlights an acute issue of "stereotyping" and "homogenization" where an individual act is ascribed as the contribution and representational mindset of the entire community.

The Muslims are always suspected and scrutinized for acts which involve terrorism and vandalism. The discourse created about them actually puts them into the picture of being someone vicious and riotous. They are quite devoted and inflexible about their religion and this adherence erroneously earns them the name of fanatics. The major problem of terrorism is attributed upon their head, for their fanaticism. In India the Muslims, with the prejudiced lenses, are seen as the "others"—religiously, culturally and socially:

> Indian Muslims are names not merely of social groups but of entire cultural and political problematics and trajectories; names, furthermore, of the respective torments of...Indian Modernity. (Mufti, 2006, 78)

They are unduly suspected in India for the mere reason that a separate state of Pakistan was asked for the security of their future during the independence phase in 1947. They have always been looked upon with paranoia, thereby, distrusting them overall. They are also typically referred to as *Pakistanis* in India, despite the fact that they made their choice to retain the

Indian identity after partition. "Drive them out" (169)! has often been the most common words heard—vocally or symbolically—against them whenever there is certain religious turbulence. In this way their survival in India is strenuous as they have to prove throughout their life that they are "true" Indians. So the major question also comes into the picture about their stance in secularism and modernity: "If "Muslim outright," then how can he be an Indian in the modern sense? And if 'no Muslim' at all, then why not a 'bare and blank' citizen?" (Mufti, 80).

Muslims are generally considered to be conservative and bigots. This point generally emanates from the point of view of their lifestyle and prayer procedure. Amin poses the question about the possibility of their being "Muslim and secular" too. He further goes on to ask questions representing differences in India, "How can difference be represented without stereotyping the group concerned" (3)? In other words, the identity of a particular community is mainly dependent on the difference and exclusion from the other. In this attempt the mainstream does not fail to demonize the other by blatantly casting aspersions on them. In the beginning of the play the Hindu chorus/Mob shouts:

CHORUS 1, 2, 3. This is our land!

How dare they?

CHORUS 1. It is in their blood!

CHORUS 1, 3. It is in their blood to destroy! (168)

Whatsoever be the contention, until and unless matters are scrutinized from a very neutral angle a right analysis is not possible. If the evaluation system itself is saturate with preconceived notions then it becomes quite difficult to keep the neutral angle intact. In the play the Muslim Chorus tries to prove its innocence:

CHORUS 1. Their chariot fell in our street!

CHORUS 2. Their God now prostrates before us!

CHORUS 3. So they blame it on us?

CHORUS 1. Was the chariot built by us?

CHORUS 2, 3. Blame the builder of those fancy thrones.

CHORUS 4. A manufacturing defect!

The Mob in the play, which is also the representative figure of the crowd in real life, shows the ingrained hatred—the Hindu Mob is mistrustful about the Muslims and vice versa. Dattani tries to put this issue high upon the mirror so that people can see and understand the real shortcomings that lead to such acrimonious situations.

From the contention above we see that politics has been inextricably pervasive in influencing the overall sphere of the society. With politics as a historical background, we perceive that a distorted notion is played upon the question of representation of Muslims in India. The question of representation has always been a biggest bone of contention. The percentage of verisimilitude that one finds in representation can always be questioned upon. The Muslims have been represented as a "minority" and therefore, "underdeveloped":

> It is, rather, the symptom of a crisis—and, to be precise, of a crisis of representation—within the experience of Indian nationhood itself: the (nationalist) claim for the existence of a singular Indian nation (state) seeks to place "the Muslims" in the place of the national minority.... So whereas the majority (culture) is implicitly recognized as being internally structured by class, that is, as constituting a social whole, the minority is cast as segment only, and becomes an undifferentiated staging ground for the traditional, the pre-modern, the underdeveloped, the archaic. (Mufti, 84-85)

The Muslims by themselves are capable and talented individuals. They are certain sectors which have not been too favourable to them, in trusting them with jobs and other valid rights. On the other hand, even the Muslims choose not to get exposed to modern systems. However, the failure of "the Moslems" to fully experience modern life is not due to "innate failing," but to "historical causes" (Mufti, 81). Moreover, being a minority group they are always expected to adhere to the majority rules, in the process of which they have to adopt many things:

> The discourse of minorities, spoken for and against in the multicultural wars, proposes a social subject constituted through cultural hybridization, the over-determination of communal or group differences, the articulation of baffling alikeness and banal divergence. (Bhabha, 1996, 54)

This "hybridization" can be seen under various lime-lights. It can be seen as something which brings cultures together, thereby increasing the potential to open-mindedness and feeling of benevolence. There would also be cultural exchanges in terms of patterns of living and thinking as proposed in the idea "unity in diversity." However, when we analyse the wider gamut of reflection, i.e. the majority view of the minority, we find this "unity" losing its trace in thin air. No diversity is countenanced unless 'they' appear different to 'us' in the way 'we' expect them to (Amin, 2005, 169). Consequently, the only remnants that can be found are dregs of hatred and intolerance which shakes the notion of 'unity'.

The notion of hatred is also brew by the representational phase which has certain political gimmick underneath which compels us to question the sacrosanct limitations of both—religion and politics. The modern state requires a pristine boundary between different ideological apparatus of the State like politics, economy, religion, etc. Nonetheless this is a utopian idea as one is integrally bound to the other, in its functioning and its growth. Even then the proper co-ordination can be maintained in the mutual functioning of these diverse institutions within a state for which the State mechanism needs to play a crucial and justified role. This puts into the picture the involvement of human machinery—politicians. What or how do the politicians retain their hold in the modern secular state? What are the methods they adopt? What are the gimmicks they uphold to come to power? Does this ensure a stable secular state or do they rather fragment the people on religion based issues? All these queries become quite inevitable to know the play of power-politics, and the stance of secular identity.

In the contemporary time, politicians have earned malice over their reputation by indulging over maters which go against the public benefit. Masses become mere plaything in their hand and a medium to stage them in power. Smita in *Final Solutions* brings to the limelight the real face of the politicians who ruthlessly and remorselessly engage in evil acts. She says that it is the politicians who are the real culprits who hoodwink innocent people and misuse the youths. Her hatred towards them is stark when she unveils a fact about Javed and tells that politicians "hire" him [implicating, the goons] in order to create violence:

> SMITA (to Ramnik). They hire him! They hire such people!
>
> RAMNIK. They who?
>
> SMITA. Those...parties! They hire him! That's how he makes a living. They bring him and many more to the city to create riots. To...throw the first stone! (195)

The politicians provoke the Hindus against the Muslims and the vice versa. They do so to keep their vote-bank intact. The politicians secure votes in the name of religion, community, caste and other such social 'artefact'. Religion is thoroughly discussed by them in the public sphere. Asad's question becomes vital here: "If the adherents of a religion enter the public sphere, can their entry leave the pre-existing discursive structure intact?" For this question Asad himself replies "no":

> The public sphere is not an empty space for carrying out debates. It is constituted by the sensibilities—memories and aspirations, fears and hopes—of speakers and listeners.... Thus the introduction of new discourses may result in the disruption of the established assumptions structuring debates in the public sphere. (185)

So the major question is to see how the public sphere is used. Who is playing upon the voice of the masses? How do the mass homogenise these spaces? And who creates this hegemony within them? When the chorus in the play openly vent their anger it reflects their "pre-existing" anguish and their "sensibility". For the masses the space for rationality becomes blurred when the question involves matters relating their faith and emotion.

They cannot be pacified with whatsoever amount of effort. For instance, the Muslim Chorus asserts that the Hindus and Muslims are destined to be forever at loggerheads and that they can never be one (Prasad, 90):

> CHORUS 1. Should we be swallowed up? Till they cannot recognize us? Should we melt into anonymity, so they cannot hound us? Lose ourselves in a shapeless mass? Should We? Can We? (196)

We know through their voice that they are being exploited and their innocence is being misused by people in authority. This also brings us to understand the nasty way in which the politics operates. The leaders do not mind hoodwinking the common people to keep their vote-bank intact and to grab power and embezzle money.

Baa/Hardika always remains under the impression that her father was killed by the Muslims. She lives with that thought throughout her life. However, when Ramnik relates the fact to her that her father and husband had burnt down the Muslim shop so that they could purchase it at half its value, Hardika gets horrified. She comes to realize that her years of hostility towards the Muslims were an outcome of mere misunderstanding. Ramnik did not want to go to the shop because of his guilt feeling. He pleads with Javed to take up the job in the shop in order to recompense a bit of that guilt. However, Javed does not take the job. There is a display of complete distrust among the two communities, replicated through these two individuals:

> RAMNIK. Why do you distrust us?
>
> JAVED. Do you trust us?
>
> RAMNIK. I don't go about throwing stones!
>
> JAVED. But you do something more violent. You provoke! You make me throw stones! Every time I look at you my bile rises! (198)

We come to realize that though Ramnik puts on the secular face, but there is a history of subterfuge and compromise within it. Bobby's statement, "... I was ashamed of being myself" (91) elicits a response from him, "We are not very different, are we"

(91)? Both of them were caught in the lurch between social conformity and individual conscience. "They are torn between a sense of fidelity towards their religion, the ideas and ideals of the people of their own community and a sense of what is right" (Prasad, 91). We do come to realize that even if individuals want to carve out their own distinct way of living and their own identity they are always scrutinized by society. Hence they can have no solution to their problem of difference, because in order to formulate and wend one's way the use of agency is limited to a great extent. The cultural factor goes ahead to determine the identity to a great degree.

Smita is an epitome of a secular and modern figure who makes an attempt to reconcile the Orthodox religious tension and the modern paradigm of livelihood. Her understanding and maturity provides hope for the audience that a positive light is still on among people, who are tolerant and accepting in full catholicity. She understands the problems of the minorities and also knows her mother's dominant and entrenched ideology that her mother Aruna had internalized patriarchal order so deep that she wanted to inject her with the same, as it was the ultimate truth for her:

> ARUNA. What makes you think you have all the answers? Don't you have any respect for who you are? I shudder to think, what will become of your children? What kind of sanskar will you give them when you don't have any yourself? It's all very well to have progressive ideas. But you are progressing or are you drifting? God knows, I don't want all this violence. How can I, when I won't even harm a goat or a chicken?... (210)

Smita does not resist to what her mother says. At the same time she also does not prefer to engross herself in "Poojas" and religious duties like her mother. She is educated and liberal. Her liberal notion keeps intact the idea of *live and let live*. She gets so shocked when her father interrogates her for showing her acquaintance with the two boys—Javed and Babban. She simply cannot believe that her father would be so interrogative on such a petty issue, and the whole pedestal of secularism and liberal notion that her father, Ramnik, had been projecting collapses before her eyes.

Smita on the other hand does not go on displaying her liberalism just to project herself ethically just. It is towards the end of the play that she displays her sense of liberalism of which her father had been putting on the mask. She thus, gives reason for not showing her secularism earlier:

> Because...because it would have been a triumph for you—over mummy. And I couldn't do that to her. And I couldn't do that to her. (Aruna is visibly moved by this remark to Ramnik). How easy it would have been for us to join forces and make her feel she was wrong. How easy to just push her over because you will have me telling her exactly what you wanted to tell yourself. (To Aruna) What would you have done? Shut yourself from us? We wouldn't let you off so easily. We would've hounded you. We wouldn't've let you forget that the spirit of liberalism ran in our blood and that you were the oddity—you were the outsider! What would happen to you then? How weak and frustrated would you feel! You do get what I mean, don't you, mummy? (213-14)

We see certain changes in the environment towards the end of the play. Aruna enters after a bath and starts her daily Pooja when she starts ringing the Pooja bell, Javed and Babban advance towards her. In spite of her protests Bobby enters the Pooja room and picks up the image of Lord Krishna very delicately and respectfully. He wanted to prove that the Hindu gods did not consider them as idol breakers and were not angry and prejudiced against them. He says:

> Your god! My flesh is holding Him! Look, Javed! And He does not mind!
>
> * * * *
>
> Look how He rests in my hands! He knows I cannot harm Him. He Knows His strength! I don't believe in Him but He believes in me. He smiles! He smiles at our trivial pride and trivial shame. (224)

This act bridges the gulf that the feeling of distrust had produced till that time and makes the characters look over each other in their intention and not mere action. There was a pristine sanctity in the intention of Bobby who overcomes distrust through trust and open-heart.

"In order for a society to be modern it has to be secular and for it to be secular it has to relegate religion to non-political spaces because that arrangement is essential to modern society" (Asad, 182). I believe that one undergoes a broader challenge to maintain a secular state. The challenge emanates from various quarters. The stance of secularism on itself would require it to be more feasible on the political front at the same time on the religious front too. In the secular environment, there needs to be a scope for "free speech" with its "physical ability to speak" and "to be heard" (184). However, given the fact that in India there are numerous religions and multi-lingual diversities, they preclude the possibility of any solution. The nation-state is supposed to be a secular entity, and religious nationalism within it always comes up as a challenge and threat to some extent. A whole lot of incompatibility is perceived between modern life and Islamic values; however it is also a matter of faith and adherence. The constitutional freedom should prepare the ground which somehow leads to the peaceful functioning of all these either in public or in private space.

The public space has turned out to a battlefield in *Final Solutions* where there is an open slandering of reputation, hurling of abuses in the street. There is no chance of peaceful negotiation. The mob is widely played upon by some hidden political agenda, of which they themselves are ignorant, therefore, they flow with the tide. There is a paradoxical claim of final *solutions* where one solution would never come to save anything; therefore, the word "final" itself is a great fiasco. It is like the infinite process of transcendental signified where the centrality of the solution keeps on moving. At the same time the solution which would be dependent on fulfilment of some other condition and this would go on prolonging interminably. There is a requirement of a whole series of solutions, which might or might not be met, depending upon the feasibility of chance. The final scene in the Pooja room might be a way to initiate the process of peace-talk, where differences are removed and then individuals get into the same plane. Even to do that a whole lot of courage of conviction, painstaking effort and risk-taking determination is required.

Conclusively, we can say that there is a rescue point in Smita who is an epitome of a secular figure—tolerant, understanding, educated, modern and mature. In order to have a more open space for secularism to flourish one has to shed one's entrenched prejudices at the same time one needs to be educated to the point of maturity, of thoughts and beliefs. Even internalization of old prejudices is quite dangerous for the existence of secularism. The essence of secular space depends upon how the "self" co-relates in terms of the "others". There might not be a spectacular final solution to the problems of religious strife unless certain fundamental elements of well-being like trust and love can shrink a whole lot of ensconced hatred from society. The temple case in Gandhi's house towards the end of the drama anticipates a lot of positive hope, where there is a transcending of cultural boundary and trust mitigates perfidious ambience. The other section of the society, like political, may try to divide and rule over people through their propaganda. Nonetheless, the people have to come in terms of understanding the ground reality by educating themselves and keeping their eyes open.

Too much of religious adherence makes each and every individual quite adamant, and reaches to the extent of being fanatic about his/her own religion. When people from the same religion or section of society undergo the same circumstances they raise a platform of uniformity where they act as a collective whole. This collective whole generates certain common feelings which lead to the consensual ground among them. When they take some decision for or against by persuading or propelling others from similar faith or situations a mass hysteria is spawned. Mass hysteria has been a major factor in the evocation of a collective identity. A group of a particular faith, religious or cultural, drives other people of the same faith to act in a particular way, often hoodwinking, to some deeds—the Mob/ Chorus in the play. Many people who are lead by the mass hysteria are themselves innocent and ignorant. In such situation it is quite difficult to retain one's individuality, to stand for the courage of one's conviction.

Hence there is a requirement of multiple solutions, therefore, the apt title of the play *Final Solutions* because one or some solutions will not suffice. The questions of Minority, Secularism and Modernity have been subtly touched by Dattani who leaves for his audience to react and analyse. Trust and distrust becomes a major benchmark which decides the sustenance of diverse faiths, religions and even other kinds of relation collaboratively. This play still retains a universal appeal and works as a fulcrum which holds and orchestrates major problems of society.

Works Cited

Amin, Shahid. "Representing the Musalman: Then and Now, Now and Then." *Subaltern Studies XII: Muslims, Dalits and the Fabrications of History*. Ed. S. Mayaram, M.S.S. Pandian and Ajay Skaria. Delhi: Permanent Black & Ravi Dayal Publisher, 2005. 1-35. Print.

Asad, Talal. "Secularism, Nation-State and Religion." *Formations of the Secular: Christianity, Islam, Modernity*. New York: Stanford University Press, 2003. 181-201. Print.

Bhabha, Homi K. "Cultures' In-between." *Questions of Cultural Identity*. Eds. Stuart Hall and Paul Du Gay. London: Sage, 1996. 53-60. Print.

Chandhoke, Neera. "Approaching Minority Rights: Some Perspectives." *Beyond Secularism*. New Delhi: OUP, 2000. 80-114. Print.

Chatterjee, Partha. "Secularism and Toleration." *A Possible India: Essays in Political Criticism*. New Delhi: OUP, 1997. 228-62. Print.

Das, Sangeetha. "The Sensational Issues in the Plays of Mahesh Dattani." *The Commonwealth Review*, 13.2 (2004): 51-59. Print.

Dattani, Mahesh. *Collected Plays*. New Delhi: Penguin Books, 2000. Print.

Mufti, Amir R. "Secularism and Minority: Elements of a Critique." *Social Texts*. 45(Winter 1995) 75-96. *JSTOR*. Web. 23 Mar 2006.

Padamsee, Alam. "A Note on the Play." *Collected Plays* by Mahesh Dattani. New Delhi: Penguin, 2000. Print.

Prasad, Amar Nath. *The Dramatic W orld of Mahesh Dattani: A Critical Exploration*. New Delhi: Sarup Book Pub., 2009. Print.

Veer, Peter Van Der. *Imperial Encounters: Religion and Modernity in India and Britian*. Delhi: Permanent Black, 2001. Print.

6

Interrogating Social Conscience: Re-reading Dattani's *Where Did I Leave My Purdah?*, *The Big Fat City* and Karnad's *Wedding Album*

Soumyadip Ghosh

Really what keeps us apart
At the end of years is unshared
childhood...
...Probably
Only the Egyptians had it right:
their kings had sisters for queens
to continue the incests of childhood into marriage.
Or we should do as well-meaning,
...carry marriage back into the namelessness of childhoods.

—A.K. Ramanujan, *Love Poem for a Wife I*

Modern Indian English Drama, with its various layers of themes, seeks to drag out the essence of drama from the fulcrum of the high promise of colonial era, often designed with sensationalism of romanticism and nationalism. As a matter of fact, it seeks to delineate the position of a being, undergoing various facets of suffering and torments yet is able to define its own location by acquiring a sense of prominence interfaced with consciousness. The hiatus between what the man craves to be and what he really is leads to his identity crisis but the crisis is resolved by the characters themselves, by dint of their own urge to fight against the odds of the society and machinery. Thus, their fighting becomes a site of clash and confrontation between so-called 'normative' and 'non-normative'. Aparna Bhargava Dharwadker in her article "The Critique of Western Modernity in Post-Independence India" argues:

> The critique of modernity in Indian theatre is therefore, riddled with inconsistency, misrepresentation, and contradiction. Yet by creating a hierarchy of cultural forms and negating certain forms of theatre, this critique has effectively obscured the actualities of post-independence theatre.... (qtd. in Bhatia, 73)

In a decolonised society like Indian one, the genre called 'theatre' is essentially complex in its liaison to tradition and modernity and it also creates the ambiguity by way of the entailment of multiplicity, variety and cultural heterogeneity within it. Regarding the mode of workability of Post-Independence Indian theatre, P. Obula Reddy observes, "Despite macro-political efforts to forge a single, pan-Indian 'national culture' based on a national identity, actual process of cultural representation since Independence reflects an effort to gain a sense of identity independent from that of the colonised 'British Subject'" (qtd. in Reddy and Dhawan, 34). Hence, dramatists like Mahesh Dattani and Girish Karnad went back and sometimes delved deep into the mass bases of Indian society to retrieve essential Indian social tools and taboos already always prevalent, may be in latent form in Indian social conscience and thereby questioning the efficacy of those tools make their play scripts a token of trans-historical inter-culturalism. If analysis is made on some selective plays by Dattani such as *Where Did I Leave My Purdah?*, *The Big Fat City* and Karnad's *Wedding Album*, one may be at a position to decipher that these plays put a glimpse into such socially hidden issues that might have been existing in Indian psyche but unfortunately they have never given such importance so as to make their way on to both Page and Stage. The treatment of social issues as done by both Dattani and Karnad in their plays, of course, gives birth to a new social class which is conscious of its own authenticity yet never in a position to forget its conflated history. The emergence of this new social class is truly a result of the endeavour of the playwrights who did so, as opines Nandi Bhatia, "by redefining the modern in ways that recognized the modern and the traditional, the urban and the rural, and the classic and the folk as being mutually influencing and inseparable" (Bhatia, xxiv).

Mahesh Dattani's *Where Did I Leave My Purdah?* (2014) is a play which shows how the playwright interrogates and negotiates with the issues of society and how from an almost void like situation an artist persists with her dream in favour of producing a play and thereby the play becomes a site of contestation of various social and personal motives and desires. Similarly, in *The Big Fat City* (2014), Dattani provides a series of possibilities to identify the identities of modern Indians. The play, based on the issue of delineating the void in urban figures, offers the continuous hardship that human beings undergo in a given crisis. The couple Murli and Niharika in the play fail to cope up with the need of the hour and hence, arises the dichotomy between the desire of individual beings and what they are indeed provided with. In this way, Dattani seeks to challenge the social inefficacy with which individuals survive with and in process tries to justify the cause of the ennui, a human mind bears, so much so the ultimate resistance human figures provide, is nothing but the result of incompatibility between the societal norms with which they are almost forcefully bound and the compassion they feel for themselves is at the cost of being unable to cope up with the social tradition. On the other hand, Karnad's *Wedding Album* (2008) shows the discord of marital harmony as a genesis of nuptial disruption and how the changing mentality of the contemporary Indian society interrogates age old rituals and customs related to these. Thus, in a nutshell, these plays present and represent several issues related to society and individual which give provision of the making and surfacing of the new birth of characters in terms of their growth of psyche. Karnad himself remarks, "The basic concern of the Indian theatre in the post-independence period has been to try to define its 'Indianness'" (qtd. in Multani, 35). Propagation of ethnic India at the world theatre is a prominent strategy of decolonization. Asha Kuthari Chaudhuri, in this respect observes:

> In creating and locating the self and constructing the identities of the characters who people his theatre, Dattani seems to contribute to the matrix of the processes that Erin Mee refers to as 'a way of decolonizing the theatre' without, however, resorting to 'a politically driven search for an indigenous aesthetics and dramaturgy.' (Chaudhuri, 75)

It is somewhat superfluous to locate to, what extent the overlapping of page and stage into a single artefact enhances the psyche of the readers because if we look at the plays such as *Where Did I Leave My Purdah?* and *The Big Fat City,* we sense how the episteme of modern naturalistic theatre colludes with the imperatives of postcolonialism to render an assemblage of modernity with layers of social conscience. The inception of this process of entailing a constant paradigm into a theatrical generic pattern remains somewhat absent in Indian stage before the apparition of Dattani whose *Where Did I Leave My Purdah?* and *The Big Fat City* epitomise a fine and soothing balance between the two and therefore, the page becomes a part of stage and vice versa; the criss-crossing of modern and postcolonial methods so as to be a potent means of the act of deniability to any stabilised format makes the plays unique in nature and tone. Indeed, the plays suffice Dattani's contribution to literary scene, as observes Parmar, "...when Indian Drama in English was passing through the dearth of dramas especially dramas with worth stage ability" (qtd. in Prasad, 155). Indeed, Dattani is both a man of and on the theatre and the cohesive message of his texts get self-reflexivity by means of the innovative devices he employed on the stage because to him "dramatic representation is neither a matter of the description nor of presentation but it is a matter of evocation" (Prasad, 30).

Bijay Kumar Das marks that, "Dattani's themes strike us for two reasons—novelty and authenticity. Therein lays his strength and the hallmarks of his achievement" (Das, 60). So far as the title of Dattani's play *Where Did I Leave My Purdah?* is concerned, it seems that the term 'purdah' has been employed as a trope for the act of layering, layers put on the dramatic personae for their feeling of separation from the past and therefore, despite staying very much in present, the characters have the accessibility to go to the past in favour of dragging the experience from the past to bring them into present to make comparison between the two elemental status to critique the present because the lacuna inherent in the present cannot be defined as potent devices to be redefined until and unless it has been put into a comparison with the past. In the play, *Where Did I Leave My Purdah?*, we find Nazia Sahiba, a self-absorbed diva whose life and work include several decades of political upheavals. Nazia is a yester-year theatre actress who comes to India after partition with the intention and wish to pursue her love for theatre. In the play-within-play, *Shakuntala* where Suhel and Nazia play lovers both off and on the stage, is a metaphor for Nazia's own tussled life. King Dushyant in "Shaku", a postmodern image of Kalidasha's classic, forgets his beloved Shakuntala and her love for him because of a curse upon her; but in Dattani's play it is Nazia herself who proposes to forget her own traditions and family in Lahore. The purpose of these modifications in the classic themes and structure is to break into the theatre movement which Dattani himself confesses:

> My milieu is theatre. You can't operate in isolation.... I do want a theatre movement to happen...we have talent, but theatre is more than that, it is a craft communicating through language of action. (qtd. in Agarwal, 185)

The inversion of the act of performing provides the forget-ability which is here installed in the figure of a female that acts both as an inversion of the canon in suggesting that the authenticity of any alteration must not necessarily be associated with only a male as well as a resistance to the normative behavioural pattern of patriarchy.

Dattani's *Where Did I Leave My Purdah?* is often considered to be a play full of love, compassion, humour, betrayal, envy, jealousy and grief and the dramaturgy shows the trajectory of a psyche fissured by both the victimisation of separation from her lover and as well as a victimisation of partition. Hence, the personal (in the form of jolt) and the interpersonal (framed within a nationalist issue) imperatives are put into a single self coupled with ennui and repression. Nazia is a faded theatre diva of 1950s musical theatre and founder of the fabled theatre group The Modern Indian Theatre which metonymically signals out towards IPTA and Naya Theatre. In her performance she was famed for portraying the mythical Shakuntala, seduced and abandoned by king Dushyant, and she is now reduced to granny roles in mainstream film. Gauri Shankar Jha, in this concern, observes, "Dattani unconsciously hints at the plight of women, torn between being and becoming" (qtd. in Jha, 197). A layer which is created in the life of Nazia by the experience she witnessed and suffered and her entire endurance becomes the episteme in her life by which she progresses towards a more specific version of self both as a female figure as well as a female 'artist'.

Nazia is both a victor and victim of given crisis. Initially she was oppressed by the dominant norms of the society but as she progresses towards the maturity in life she learns to resist the various forms of torture and this has been aptly dramatised by Dattani through gestures on the stage. Thus, in *Where Did I Leave My Purdah?*, Dattani very eloquently dramatises the psyche of a feminine self who becomes the figure of the multiple facets in life but never gives up the artistic idea which she owns as her own. The aesthetic creativity in her never dies and for this she even carries the memories of the horrible scenes of partition, brutal rape of her sister, separation from her lover, she is at once, at work to procure a play in her own version interpreting the canon. Even in a Naturalistic Theatre, the dramatist allowed his character to bring back the past by way of remembering the oppressed memories of the past. Therefore, Nazia becomes a figure who lives in present but survives through past. She, in process, turns out to be an 'interpreter of her own maladies'. The theatrical variety which Dattani creates by way of blurring the rigidity between naturalistic and expressionistic versions of theatre proposes the newness he was about to bring into the traditional concept of Indian theatre.

Where Did I Leave My Purdah? is a play about a Muslim actress who has an epiphany on a film set. The director wants to restrict her to a line but she realizes this space is too narrow for her to negotiate. Therefore, she finds the moment crucial for her to go back to the epic stage musicals of 1950s so much so she puts herself in a position to ensure the fact that she never gets deprived from tasting the real essence of art. In the play, the word 'Purdah' has been used by Dattani as a metaphor for all types of barriers resulting into separation. The extent of separation is also patent between men and women the 'Purdah' also plays the role of the veil of personal modesty that an actor has to give up for the sake of performance on the stage. Lillete Dubey summarises the kernel idea of the play stating it a play based on "a story set against the backdrop of the theatre, tracing some of the theatrical forms that constitute our history, and recounting a tale that mirrored the stories of a multitude of women artistes who were consumed with a love for their craft, almost at the cost of everything else" (Dattani, *Me and My Plays*, 48).

In *The Big Fat City*, Mumbai has been shown as a city of destroyer of lives and where relationships die for a quite non-viable cause. The couple Murli and Niharika in the play and their inherent difference of attitude towards life shows the dichotomy in urban peoples' psyche. Murli who had been laid off is dumped by feelings of declining self worth and his wife Niharika who has been over-conscious by the phobia of losing home becomes hard eyed to have prosperity in life. The difference of behaviour between the figures sharing the same room climaxes the contrasting imperatives prevalent in human mind. Niharika arranges a dinner party for Sailesh, Murli's college mate, whom she falsely believes in doing well for the couple. She also ropes in a neighbour, a glamorous television actress who was also suffering from her own financial troubles. After the television star's husband is killed accidentally by the passionate lover of the young paying-guest living at Murli's apartment, it changes into a space for a general unravelling of the tension existed and created in the play by way of showing various layers of tenets in individual characters. Murli consistently overacts, yet his wife, Niharika, is allowed to be a hollow portrait of an averagely greedy woman representing an average being's dream of success while staying at a metro-city.

The reference to a police raid during a neighbour's party, an oblique reference to Ekta Kapoor for showing the status of a television star who needs to work hard to be stable at state, and mention of *Haryana Khap Panchayat* to make a sense of a pan-Indian feeling work as labels of cultural void and failure of contemporary individuality at work in *The Big Fat City*. As Achint Kaur in "A Note on the Play" writes, "These are values that may shock us in the city and yet might help us question our own ethos-something that the play, in turn, compels its audience to do" (qtd. in Dattani, *Me and My Plays,* 149). The inclusion of bad taste through the reference to the tragedy of a woman in terms of her jumping from the roof, which is a quite relevant practice in a metro-city, can also be perceived in the play. So, the brilliant fusion of social issues and fractured selves of characters makes the play a unique one on Indian stage where the surfacing of new characters with new dimensions of identity can be located because the play is again based on urban scenario and the clash of inner realties pushes a being to the limit transgressing the aesthetics of stereotypical gender perversion which is generally located with the phallus but in this case the greedy depiction of Niharika makes it clear that pervasive desire is independent of gendered self. Indeed, *The Big Fat City* regulates and generalises "a form of drama which displays a marked disillusionment and cynicism. It shows human beings without convictions and with little hope, regulated by fate, or fortune or incomprehensible powers" (qtd. in Cuddon, 87).

Thus, both *Where Did I Leave My Purdah?* and *The Big Fat City* reveal that Mahesh Dattani's position in relation to the trajectory of Indian English Drama is not only determined by the changes brought about by him in the theatricality, so to say changes on 'stage' but also with the imperatives he drew, both as a playwright and a wisher of driving away social taboos in a hetero-normative societal structure, and exposed in and through his writings and therefore, via 'page'. Obviously, the immediate question which strikes a critical mind on the ground of newness brought about by Dattani through his plays is all about the exposition and explication of issues which yet remain un-attempted in page and on stage as well as for the Indian context is concerned. "The subjects of his plays not only reflect life but they deal with life head on" (Dhawan and Pant, 119). In his articulation of the themes, Mahesh Dattani is simultaneously careful and conscious so as to make his write up aware of the contemporary Indian scenario and therefore, even if when he deals with issues like the nostalgia of an actress and different layers consciousness, born out of contestation against the societal codes and norms, in her character as may be found in *Where Did I Leave My Purdah?* or the angst in urban minded people to float with the tide of traditional social patterns and any subversion into it create the entire disruption in psyche which has been shown eloquently in *The Big Fat City*. Dattani treats the themes with frankness exploiting the hollowness of culture and monolithicity of the governing forces of the society. Out of this tussle between the oppressors and oppressive, centralised and marginalised what ultimately surfaces at the tools of the representation is the birth of an identity which had to suffer at its blossom for gaining the ground but at last through various struggles and toleration of oppression it gets its due cognition. This process of the birth of this new identity which is essentially individual yet a product from various social conflations creates the plays as somewhat postcolonial because the identity is a formed one and necessarily got the consciousness through the battles fought on itself.

Human relationship and its subtle complexities find candid outlet in Girish Karnad's *Wedding Album* which critiques the ongoing essentialism of Hindu middle-class family and an account of the modern mythic hermeneutics of a forthcoming marriage in the middle-class, Karnataka based Saraswat family-the Nadkarnis. In the play marriage has been presented in its dissonant forms and hailed only as "a gamble. No escaping the fact, marriage is a gamble" (Scene IX, 89). In fact, the play, in terms of its title, is referential to that of marriage and issues related to it; the society represented by the playwright becomes a passive tool of perceiving the trajectory of the evolution of marriage in Indian society which interrogates the role of efficacy of the solemnity attached to the ritual and this act of questioning targets at the projection of the constant disruption of a so-called legitimised institution. Karnad in the play seems to question the validity of the foundation of the marriage system seen through the stereotypical eyes of the family which accepts marriage as a workplace of the two different souls to be united in the presence of the ritual enchantment rather the playwright envisages the thought of new woman who not only engages herself to the domain of marriage as a sole member to maintain its autonomy but also a figure who has her own works in a completely separate zone determined by herself. The contesting ideas of a working lady whose self is fissured and fractured by the personal and impersonal domain make the very crux of the play quite dynamic and diachronic. The inference of patriarchy as a body to control and legitimise the entire enduring performance of a woman as a loyal cum committed wife, if not, spouse is presented as an ontological crisis faced by an Indian wife in the play and the dissatisfaction emerging out of the 'tortured' motif experienced by a woman is reflected in the words of Hema, "...the white wife refuses to go trailing after her husband. We Indian women, on the other hand, are obedient Sati Savitris, ever willing to follow our husband's footsteps.... Our men may get all the top jobs. But I am in better position than Ma" (Scene 2, 17). Sharma puts it,

> The women characters look out for companionship in the play as Karnad marks the relative absence of the approval, acceptance and physical closeness which leads to deprivation and insecurity in marital relationship. The deprivation is subtly hidden in varied relations shown in the play, for the characters involved are preoccupied with themselves and their jobs. (Sharma, 4)

In the play, the social imperatives are made synonymous with the rites and rituals, social class, racial backgrounds which are also mingled with physical beauty, intellectual prowess, social aptness and an ideal couple would always look to bring about the maximum efficacy of these to maximise their nuptial prosperity.

In fact, the expected consent from a parent is matter of proliferation in the play such as we find the consent coming from Rohit's father in the matter choosing life-partner and the play further problematises the issue of choosing partner from the same community violation of which is considered to be an offence in a typical Hindu family. In the words of Sharma, "The blatant blindness of the choice and the ambiguity of the outcome of the marriage have been defined in the play through Vidula's and Ashwin's marriage" (Sharma, 5). The couples in the play such as Vidula Nadkarni and Ashwin Panje, Rohit and Tapasya, Pratibha and Irfan, Hema and Chandrakant, Mother and Father do reflect the construction of pair in terms of the mutual collaboration of thoughts and wavelength yet resulting into individual outcome of opinions. The relationships presented in the play are also not devoid of the parallel growth of the act submission and domination and the complexity arising out of the apparatus is often shown to lead towards the physical violence as well. Sharma was no wrong while saying,

> ...characters in the play are seen as survivors for they have failed to meet their Partner's psychological needs. The intimate relationship fails to allow the spouses to come together to receive and devote themselves to each other. The partial and incomplete negotiations in the various phases of marriage further lead to marital failure in the play. Karnad questions the capacity of the partners to deal with difficulties and ultimately presents the risk of failure that is increased with passing time. (Sharma, 8)

In a nutshell, Karnad's *Wedding Album* shows the marital disorder and disharmony resulting into the failure and disruption of any marital relationship. In the words of Amrit Srinivasan,

> *Wedding Album* walks a razor's edge in seeking to convey South Indian Brahmin marriage's remarkable and culturally unique contribution to Indian global success, without at the same time shying away from exposing the excruciating, even obscene risks involved in its transnational undertaking...women's emotional pain and self-endurance is voiced at different points in the play only to underline the complete invisibility granted to such domestic sacrifice on the public plane. Marriage within the caste being synonymous with approval, the

> very publicity and correctness of it muffles and chastens women in their sexuality after marriage. (Karnad, *Wedding Album*, xv)

Vidula's ignorance in cooking or giving up taking fish while joining her husband in USA may be taken to be a site of metonymical representation of her desire to be committed to her love for her better half, despite all her arrogant and snobbish side to him. Srinivasan, in this connection, observes,

> The will to serve and subjugate herself through a life decision she has willingly made, remains metaphorically outside the kitchen but, nonetheless, a purely private resolve, invisible in its worth, even to her brother and sister. (Karnad, *Wedding Album*, xvi)

Thus, the play can be taken to be an epitome materializing the effects of marital disharmony and as a playwright, Karnad's stance is somewhat both of a critic critiquing the imperatives of traditional system of marriage resulting into a nuptial void and of a preacher who took the stance of ventilating the adversaries related to the overlapping of thoughts blurring generation gap and exalts it to the levels of boundaries related to the class, caste, race, gender and of course formation of psyche.

Both Karnad and Dattani have created figures interfaced with various traits of human nature of courage, boldness and sensitivity and in them one can sense an essence of confessional mode in so far as they create their own identity not by succumbing themselves before the odds of life but make a critique of the prevalent scenario so as to make their new identity which is both critical and ambiguous. In fact, both the dramatists are, to some extent, concerned with the act of unravelling the complexity of human character and their men and women do delineate the tendencies of the contemporary social beings dismantling the stereotypical rigidity of any social code imposed upon them in favour of constructing their identity as new men/women types. The characters, often termed to be fit into the situation, are trapped in the luminality of worldly reality and inner conception to understand that reality and social machineries keep them fixed at the very foundation of societal codes so much so any attempt to regulate either of these pulls would make them 'breakers' of any act of so-called legitimisation. They are expected to behave within the set paradigms of morality, culture, rites and rituals, modes of behaviour set for them and any violation of either of these would be considered to be offensive and hence applicable for being punished as per the standard codes of laws in the society. These facets mould their mental set up and a constant observation to keep them under the stereotyped social hegemony is set up in terms of the perceivable institutions which work simultaneously for executing power and maintaining an apparent statuesque. Nimsarkar observes, "These agencies have ensured the development of a 'superego' in consonance with cultural practices in them as members of the society" (Nimsarkar, 233).

There seems to be a point of commonality shared by the characters of *Where Did I Leave My Purdah?*, *The Big Fat City* and *Wedding Album* because in each of these plays the central crux always does centre around the society and its treatment towards the individuals. The characters do undergo, at various stages, severe treatment of harshness and rudeness employed upon them; for instance, in *Where Did I Leave My Purdah?* the bitter memories of past never get out of mind in Nazia and as a result whatever she is today, it becomes an admixture of both the past and present. Both Karnad and Dattani treat the social issues in their plays from the humanitarian points of view and the result of which gets flourished in the birth of their characters that never fears to challenge the system and codes of society. They may be the oppressed at one point of time but it is they who also bounce back with their authenticity and this act of bouncing back readily shows both their latent potency to be fit in the society and the inefficacy of the social codes which used to undervalue their potency. Hence, what appears logically is that the dramaturgical point of view in each of the plays discussed above is always already humanitarian yet it is all about hurling the shafts of attack towards the machinery of the society, a place where all men live albeit a space which can be termed as a site of continuous conflict and contestation between the men and the system, between the individual as opposed to tradition.

F.H. Heinemann puts it, "Because the very existence of man on this earth is menaced, because the annihilation of man, his dehumanization and destruction of his humanity and of all moral values is a real danger, therefore, the meaning of human existence becomes our problem" (Heinemann, 178). Characters realized that any sense of exclusion from the main stream society cannot, by any means, prove their authenticity which they need to earn on their own by putting up a resistance against the odds and therefore, creation of any utopia by means of celebrating the self-authenticity will simultaneously be a configuration of self-denial. Thus, they have to fight against the oppression staying within the given premise and this should never mean succumbing to the given but questioning it so as to make it a legitimate place. Anita Desai in an interview with Jasbir Jain rightly remarks, "I don't think anybody's exile from society can solve any problem. I think basically the problem is how to exist in society and yet maintain one's individuality rather than suffering from a lack of society and a lack of belonging..." (Desai, 15). The predicament of Nazia, Niharika or Vidula is, therefore, nothing but the outcome of being victimised by the conflicting configuration of society and its tools. Karnad "revises traditional folktales and myths in order to create heroines enmeshed in the cross roads of tradition. But he tends to present women as 'cardboard characters', as persons torn between the ideal and the pragmatic or between the illusive and the real" (qtd. in Mukherjee, 265). On the other hand, Dattani proclaims, "I am not interested in characters asking existential questions in a limbo. My characters exist in a definite space and time, in a social context that's what stimulates me. I don't focus on a message but the context is important" (qtd. in Chaudhuri, 77).

Works Cited

Agarwal, Beena. *Mahesh Dattani's Plays: A New Horizon in Indian Theatre*. Jaipur: Book Enclave, 2011.

Bhatia, Nandi. *Modern Indian Theatre: A Reader*. New Delhi: Oxford University Press, 2013.

Budholia, Om Prakash. *Girish Karnad: Poetics and Aesthetics*. Delhi: B.R. Publishing Corporation, 2011.

Chaudhuri, Asha Kuthari. *Contemporary Writers in English: Mahesh Dattani*. New Delhi: Foundation Books Pvt. Ltd, 2005.

Cuddon, J.A. (ed). *Dictionary of Literary Terms and Literary Theory*. London: Penguin Books Ltd., 2000.

Das, Bijay Kumar. *Form and Meaning in Mahesh Dattani's Plays*. New Delhi: Atlantic Publishers and Distributors Pvt. Ltd, 2008.

Dattani, Mahesh. *Me and My Plays*. New Delhi: Penguin Books India Pvt. Ltd., 2014.

Dhawan, R.K. and Tanu Pant (eds.). *The Plays of Mahesh Dattani: A Critical Response*. New Delhi: Prestige Books, 2005.

Heinemann, M.W. *Existentialism and the Modern Predicament*. New York: Harper and Brothers, 1993.

Jain, Jasbir. *Stairs to the Attic: The Novels of Anita Desai*. Jaipur: Print Well, 1987.

Jha, Gauri Shankar. *Current Perspectives in Indian English Literature*. New Delhi: Atlantic Publishers and Distributors Pvt. Ltd., 2006.

Karnad, Girish. *Wedding Album*. New Delhi: Oxford University Press, 2014.

Mukherjee, Tutun (ed.). *The Plays of Mahesh Dattani*. New Delhi: Pencraft International, 2012.

——. *Girish Karnad's Plays: Performance and Perspectives*. New Delhi: Pencraft Internationals, 2006.

Multani, Angelie (ed.). *Mahesh Dattani's Plays: Critical Perspectives*. New Delhi: Pencraft International, 2007.

Nimsarkar, P.D. *Women in Girish Karnad's Plays: A Critical Perspective*. New Delhi: Creative Books, 2009.

Pandey, Punam. *The Plays of Girish Karnad: A Study in Existentialism*. New Delhi: Sarup Book Publishers Pvt. Ltd., 2010.

Prasad, Amar Nath (ed.). *The Dramatic World of Mahesh Dattani*. New Delhi: Sarup Book Publishers Pvt. Ltd., 2012.

Ramanujan, A.K. *Collected Poems*. New Delhi: Oxford University Press, 1997.

Reddy, K. Venkata and R.K. Dhawan (eds.). *Flowering of Indian Drama: Growth and Development*. New Delhi: Prestige Books, 2005.

Sharma, Ruchi. "Marital Discord and Its Assonance in Girish Karnad's play *Wedding Album*." *Journal of Higher Education and Research Society*, 1(1), Oct 2013: 1-12.

7

Gendered Self: Postmodernist Handling of a Sensitive Issue in Mahesh Dattani's *Tara*

Samina Parvin and *Munira T.*

The name of Mahesh Dattani is taken with much respect in the history of Post-Independence Indian English drama. He is a very successful playwright as he himself admitted in an interview conducted by Erin B. Mee at the Bookery in Bangalore on August 27, 1996. He told the interviewer that he is not the only successful playwright but he has been the most successful for various reasons which include his own theatre company 'Playpen' and also a theatre background. He also says, "I'm not writing because I'm a writer [of literature], I'm writing because I have a theatre background." Besides, being a successful playwright who is known to take up sensitive issues and with experimentation in drama and theatre. He is an actor, a director and an author, all rolled into one. Taking in view the different levels of Dattani's contribution, Aparna Dharwedkar in her book *Theatres of Independence* (2006) points out, "Literary playwrights such as Utpal Dutt and Mahesh Dattani, who direct and act in their own plays, seem to achieve a relatively equable balance between word and action. Dattani came to playwriting from acting and directing experiences that had stressed group work, and, like Tendulkar he underscores the importance of practical experience in the theatre," and Aparna Dharwedkar quotes the words of Dattani himself, "because you realize that you're not writing to be read.... That the actors are going to take your script and they are going to do other things with it" (Dattani, 'Page and Stage' (qtd. in) Dharwedkar, 90).

Postmodernism, postmodernity, postmodern culture and art—all these terms are known for their peculiar traits such as inconsistencies and contradictions. Keeping these things in view postmodernist art can be considered as a collage of different styles, different forms, and different media in a single art—form as Postmodernist architecture, postmodernist music, and postmodernist literature. Before going ahead, the reason why the term postmodernist has been used above and will be used further must be pointed out by summarizing the views of Steven Connor about this difference as the term 'postmodern' is used to identify the historical period that began after World War II, but 'postmodernist' "refers to cultural works that possess stylistic features that align them with postmodernism as a structure of feeling, an episteme, rather than a chronologically defined moment" (Steven Connor in *The Cambridge Companion to Postmodernism* 2004). He further states that it is not necessary that the arts, though postmodern in historical sense must be "stylistically postmodernist." In literature, "drama" as Kerstin Schmidt in her book *Theater of Transformation: Postmodernism in American Drama* (2005) mentions, "has made ample use of postmodern features that, to different degrees, express transformative practices". She further states that although the term 'postmodern' is derived with instability and diverse opinions of critics yet "postmodern drama takes up the postmodern penchant" to explore the boundaries of dramatic experimentation. Postmodern theatre covers in itself as Eric Godie in his article "Postmodern Theatre" states, all the social, philosophical and literary features of postmodernism. It considers order meaningless and rejects it. It is like a subversive revolt against historicism and emphasizes on the process rather than the goal. Eric Godie also states that "postmodern theatre is a place of infinite possibility wrought with infinite peril". As dramatists are also a part of postmodern culture, when they write a play, they inadvertently use postmodernist dramatic techniques, and if it is pointed out to them that their plays resemble that of postmodernist drama, they may answer that they don't know how this has happened. Many a times, a play seems to resemble in its events, actions, incidents and ongoing processes in a character's mind, our own reality. This is not the reality but only pretends to be so. When the boundaries of fiction and reality are mixed and blurred, it is postmodernist drama. Even when a play is made of hybrid structure, or borrowed quotations, texts and media forms or pastiche, it smells of postmodernist drama.

In a postmodernist play, the text is told from the viewpoints or perspectives of multiple characters and it is not bound to tell a single goal—aimed story. Every character, though inserted by the dramatist to reveal the main character's importance, snatches himself from the control of central authority or of author and indulges in his/her preoccupations. And thus, reaching the climax there happens the ending of different character's lives in different ways. The text of the play often attempts to expose the fluid identity of its characters. One character participates in creating one's own identity, but is changed by the things that happen or by the events out of one's control and thus is shaped by them. In this way, one becomes a collage of identities, shaped by the deeds and actions and uncontrolled reactions done in the past, present and still to be shaped in future. This fluidity in identities breaks the personality of one into fragments. Such development in character is "considered to be the harbinger of postmodernism in theatre," as Elinor Fuchs opines. "Psychologically consistent dramatic character" has been sacrificed in favour of "fragmented, flowing and uncertain identities whose exact locations and boundaries cannot be pinpointed" (Elinor Fuchs in the essay *Death of Character*).

A simulacrum, coined by Baudrillard, which contributes to a big part of postmodernism, has displaced the fiction for reality and reality for fiction. A stage in postmodernist drama is identified as a room, living room or bed room, it is not considered by the playwright, actor, director or audience also as a stage or a space for acting, but a room or the place where particular characters are living and doing actions and speaking words as their life demands and not as stage or drama demands them to act. Therefore, fictional effect in postmodernist theatre becomes more realistic than it was in modernist theatre. Thus, postmodern theatre is a reaction to the modernist visual and conceptual unified structure and a whole production. Rather, with the idea that there is no unity in the chain of events and action of human beings, postmodern theatre is the name of producing only what one can see in one's life time and as Arnold Aronson rightly states, it is only "a seemingly vulgar and alienating collage of styles, periods and references—a very conscious lack of unity among the visual elements of a production". Thus, postmodern theatre can be the "juxtaposition of seemingly incongruous elements within the unifying structure of the stage frame..." (Arnold Aronson in his essay "Postmodern Design").

Dattani comes with experimentation and applies innovative techniques in Indian English drama that have made him a success among all. Every play is experimental, first for the themes and substances dealt and then for the techniques with which he deals with those themes in his plays. And if both of them are named as postmodernist, it will remove the lack of suitable tag for which Dattani's plays are remarkable. Themes are those "invisible issues", as the playwright himself names them, that are dealt with only one postmodernist 'seriousness' or battle against the meta narratives of truth, of power and of domination which have been rejecting and suppressing them for so many years. However, it is within the canvass of Indian urban society where the issues Dattani raises have the subaltern status.

Dattani himself talks about these confrontational issues which existed in India but were not accepted. "You can talk about feminism in a way that is accepted. But you can't talk about gay issues because that's not Indian, it does not happen here. You can't talk about a middle class housewife fantasizing about having sex with the cook or having a sex-life. That isn't Indian either that's confrontational even if it's Indian" (Interview with Erin B. Mee, *PAJ*, 1997). In the same way Dattani deals in 'Tara' with the theme of which he himself tells that:

> Tara is about Siamese twins who've been conjoined from the chest down, and I've taken the liberty of making them boy and girl twins. I think it's a play about the

> self, about the man and the woman in self, but a lot of people think of it as a play about the girl child. (Dattani in Interview with Erin B. Mee, *PAJ*, 1997)

It is the result of reader response criticism, again an outlet of postmodernism that critics have made the playwright die and interpret the play as their own understanding. Some take it as a play about gender discrimination; others relate it to the male domination and the male preferences in a patriarchal Indian society; some others find the issues of family clash or a conspiracy of a lady against the lady. Whatever it is, the playwright has successfully used the technique of mixing fiction with reality and by doing so he has also succeeded in spreading the sensitization about the gendered self. According to Dattani, the play is about the male and female part of one's self, i.e. Tara and Chandan are the two parts of the same self, but still they cannot remain conjoined as they were in their mother's womb. To exist in society, they have to be separated from each other whether or not they want to be and also, whether being separated in the suitable way as was suggested by medical experts (two legs with Tara and one leg and one limp with Chandan). The fiction here is that the playwright has made them Siamese twins which are a rare case in reality. Further, they are conjoined which again is the rarest case in reality. Dattani experimented by creating this fiction to see the reaction of the 'real' patriarchal society. Again the playwright mixes (blurs) reality with fiction to see the effect in reality. As Chandan and Tara being the two bodies, have to be separated, Dattani names this separation an emotional separation or a split in self, so that people can take notice of their forgotten selves, i.e. female self in male and male self in female without which every human is incomplete and becomes weak if separated and strong if united much like as Chandan and Tara. This treatment of the central theme around which the play revolves is very much postmodernist and gets matched with the concept of simulacra given by Baudrillard, one of the main thinkers of postmodernism.

Regarding the theatrical craftsmanship Madhvi Latha, in her scholarly paper "Dattani's Dramatic Techniques" published in the anthology *Multicultural Theatre and Drama* (2011) quotes Kasturi Khantan:

> The complex structure of these plays matches their complex and disturbing thematic quality. Dattani very often places one character at a higher level so that the play is seen from his view point. Often characters are interchanged, questions asked at one point, between two characters are answered by the conversation between two characters in another part of the stage. (Khantan (qtd. in) Latha, 125-54)

Aparna Dharwedkar includes the name of Mahesh Dattani among those urban directors who work principally in realist, absurdist, and allegorical, political and meta-theatrical modes. From the beginning of the play if the technical effect is to be seen, the stage setting can be noticed as multi-level stage consisting at different levels the different portions of the places where action is to be done. Different actions are played at different places simultaneously and the playwright does not start another scene to make a start of another action. With the collapse of modernist boundaries, as the critic Mele Yamomo in his article *Defining Postmodern Theater* states, "Postmodern theatre takes on pluralism and multiplicity in style, approach and over-all process". Again he points out the characteristics of postmodern theatre as "simultaneity" and "multi dimensionality". Dattani's multi-level setting of stage is the evidence of it. Again the play carries the parallel actions simultaneously at one time. All of the Patel family is seen at their home, at the same time Roopa is seen calling Nalini and Prema. Again Chandan, Tara and Roopa converse with one another and at the same time the audience are made to see Patel's conversation with the neighbour in the street, on the way to his office.

> TARA: He writes about people he knows.
>
> ROOPA: Really? How interesting.
>
> TARA: Yes, he is going to write a story about me.
>
> PATEL: She needs help. I am not so sure—may be some kind of therapy—or counseling.
>
> TARA: About me. Strong. Healthy. Beautiful.

> ROOPA: That's not you. That's me. He is writing a story about me. Aren't you, Chandan?
>
> CHANDAN: (seriously) Yes. You are in the story too. As the ogler.
>
> PATEL: May be I need some advice...or counseling. I don't know...whether I am prepared for the worst. (Act I, 329-30)

Multi actions have been seen above and now multi-level stage setting can be seen:

> A multi-level set. The lowest level occupies a major portion of the stage. It represents the house of the Patels. It is seen only in memory and may be kept as stark as possible. The next level represents the bedsitter of the older Chandan (referred to as Dan for clarity) in a suburb of London.... Behind, on a higher level, is a chair in which Dr. Thakkar remains seated throughout the play. On the stage level, running along the cyclorama and in an L-shape, downstage right, is the galli outside the Patels' house, which can be suggested by cross-lighting. (Act I, 323)

The play starts with Dan who according to the playwright is Chandan, living now in London without any identity to substitute his guilt over the injustice done with his sister Tara. Here two things can be pointed out. First Dan who has his own past to be memorized every time that scorns him also to the deep of his soul is also the character of the play. He tries to write a play about his sister Tara but fails. Tara's story moves only in his memories but he is unable to translate it onto a paper. Secondly, the dramatist has attempted to make his play a Meta theatre as he raises Dan at a higher level as a narrator, attempting writing the play in which he himself is a character:

> All I find every day, without fail, is the type written sheet with the title of the play, my name and address and the date. Nothing changes—except the date. (*Reads from the paper.*) *Twinkle Tara*. A Drama in Two Acts by Chandan Patel. Copyright, Chandan Patel, 93. Fishpond's Road, Toating, London. SW17 7 LJ. (Act I, 324)

Meta theatre starts with the beginning of the play as a deliberate technique of the dramatist in the disguise of Chandan's attempt to write a play. The technique works the same as 'meter' does in the poetry in Wordsworth's view to control the outflow of emotions. Moreover as mentioned above, Meta theatre is a play within the play or about the play to create a self-conscious atmosphere of the play itself. Meta theatre is also the name of direct address to the audience as Meta fiction does to its readers. Dan (Chandan) does not proceed anymore to his writing page. Only Tara's story floods his memories and the play happens to begin with it.

Original play begins with the dialogue delivery and actions delivered within the memories of Dan (Chandan) while his own attempt to write a play is suspended at the same place. The play begins to develop and the audience or readers come face to face with all the major incidents, conflicts and tensions going on in the play. Each character begins enacting the role he/she is to play. The birth of Siamese twins, their separation, Patel's mental conflict caused by unexpected challenges in his life, his conflict with his wife Bharati and Bharati's mental illness are all presented along with Roopa to whom Tara tells about the stories Chandan is going to write in future. Tara's quality that she is very strong is also clearly evident before audience/readers. But Chandan's writing of the play still does not proceed; "DAN: No! No! That won't do. I can't have all that just swimming in my mind.... I've got to make a start" (Act I, 330).

This is but the technique of Meta theatre and according to Madhvi Latha, it is the technique that the play is to be seen by the points of view of Chandan.

Another point to be noted is that Dattani has not used any traditional way to introduce his characters one by one. Even though all the characters have appeared on the stage in the first Act; they have been brought in as the need demands of them. Chandan and Tara appear while Dan is thinking of the story to be written about Tara who comes only in his memories. "A spot on the stage level. Chandan and Tara walk into it. They both have a limp, but on different legs" (Act I, 324).

> TARA: And me. May be we still are, like we've always been.... Two lives and one body in one comfortable womb. Till we were forced out...and separated. (Act I, 325)

One more example of this can be noticed when Tara, Chandan, Bharati and Patel have been busy talking about themselves, Roopa, unexpectedly has been introduced as calling to Prema from her house in 'broken Gujarati' and seems to talk to Prema's mother inside the house, whose presence has been felt but is not seen on the stage. Roopa is supposed to communicate with her about Prema but only Roopa's voice or one sided conversation is to be heard. Dattani has not bound himself to present one more character here.

Fluidity in identity is also seen in the characters of this play. Patel and Bharati have shaped themselves as they wanted in the past. Bharati has become the victim of her own decision to favour the male child which she had taken with her father and now the situations cannot be stopped from worsening. Her love for Tara and the donation of her kidney to Tara are not enough to bring any change in the condition of Tara physically and emotionally. Neither can it stop her (Bharati) from becoming insane. Patel attempts much to reform the situation and to make arrangements for his children financially and academically but all in vain. He remains alone as Chandan has refused to come back from London. So what has been done in the past cannot be undone at present. Decisions should be taken after thinking of its pros and cons. Again the life of Tara and Chandan has wasted away, not by destiny but by the decisions taken in the past. Destiny though directed by the dramatist as he is the only God of the play and of its characters, has not discriminated with the girl or the boy in that way as it has been done by parents by giving the two legs to the male child and depriving female child even though the third leg was more suitable for her. And now Tara, however she wants to shape her life in her own way by finding the ways to have a strong and independent existence in the society fails to do so because like the fluid, she has to take the shape of the pot of fragmented and emotionally and physically fractured existence bound to be so because of others' decisions.

So is with Chandan who cannot forget the guilt over the death of his sister or in more suitable words of his own feminine self to which he could not save from being wasted as he was himself a child at that time. Consequently, he has to live alone under the subversive guilt torturing him everyday in the suburb of London by changing his name and without any personal history.

'Tara' also supplies the examples of being a collage of art forms and styles of the different fields by putting them together in useful ways which can be substituted in one word 'pastiche.' The stage setting tells of a chair on the higher level of stage on which Dr. Thakkar is seated throughout the whole play. It is not to be set insignificantly. The importance of his presence begins with the use of the technique of an interview of Dr. Thakkar taken by Dan acting as the interviewer to take the interview for a TV show which is named also as the 'Marvels in the Worlds of Medicine'. Dattani does not insert an extra character to play the role of an interviewer. It is played by Dan who even does not change his place rather interview session is being held by him from the same place in darkness. There is also the same address to the audience as it is done in a real TV show:

> A television show type signature tune fades in while the spot fades out. Although Dan is interviewing Dr Thakkar, he remains where he is, in darkness. The tune ends and a spot picks up Dr. Thakkar, seated as if being interviewed in a studio. (Act I, 330)
>
> DAN: (*mock-cheerful*). Good evening, viewers, and welcome to another edition of Marvels in the World of Medicine. We have with us this evening at our studio Dr. Umakant Thakkar who has been in the news lately for his outstanding work at the Queen Victoria Memorial Hospital in Bombay.... Dr. Thakkar, could you please tell us what was so special about this surgery?
>
> Dr. Thakkar: Yes, absolutely. Surgery was their only chance of survival. You see, they were twins, conjoined from the chest down. (Act I, 330)

From now onwards Dr. Thakkar is presented as a commentator time to time on the medical part—surgery of Siamese twins.

Thus, many media forms have been blended in the play. First of all it is a play, a piece of literature and also a show to be presented on the real stage or theatre in direct contact with the audience, not as a TV show. Moreover, after an original presentation in theatre, it can be presented also through television to the Tele-audience. Within the play also, it brings a TV show in the form of an interview session and it is also made obvious that this episode is a part of an on-going series of interviews. And finally, the interview is related to the field or stream of medicine, much different from the field of literature and from the whole fictional art.

Tara is one of the most discussed and well received plays of Mahesh Dattani. It is a postmodern play not just because of its technique and its theme. It can be categorized as a postmodern play because it does not follow the traditional dramatic form of five acts. The play has only two acts without any scene. There is no unity of time, place and action. Further, the past, present and future are all juxtaposed to form a complete whole. Hence, Dattani's expertise at conceiving his plays and presenting in this form make him one of the most successful playwrights of the contemporary age.

Works Cited

Aronson, Arnold. "Postmodern Design". *Theatre Journal* 43. The John Hopkins University Press. 1991. http://www.columbia.edu/~apa4/pdfs/Aronson_pomodesign.pdf. Web. 9 Sep, 2012.

Clayton J. Whistant. *Some Common Themes and Ideas within the Field of Postmodern Thought: A Handout for HIS389*. 13 May, 2012. http://webs.wofford.edu/whisnantcj/his389/Postmodernism.pdf. Web. 20 May, 2013.

Connor, Steven. ed. *The Cambridge Companion to Postmodernism*. UK: Cambridge University Press. 2004. www.cambridge.org/9780521640527. Web. 21 Feb, 2012.

Dattani, Mahesh. "Tara". *Collected Plays*. New Delhi: Penguin Books. 2000. Print.

Dharwedkar, Aparna Bhargawa. *Theatres of Independence: Drama, Theory, and Urban Performance in India Since 1947*. New Delhi: Oxford University Press. 2006. Print.

Fuchs, Elinor. *The Death of Character: Perspectives on Theatre after Modernism*. Bloomington: Indiana University Press. 1996. Print.

Goudie, Eric. *Postmodern Theatre*. 22 Jan, 2009. *http://www.helium.com/items/1307988- post-modern-theatre*. 15 Dec, 2012. Web.

Latha, Madhavi. "Dattani's Dramatic Techniques". *Multicultural Theatre and Drama*, ed. T. Sai Chandra Mouli. New Delhi: Authors Press. 2011. Print.

Mee, Erin, B. Interview. "Mahesh Dattani: Invisible Issues." *PAJ*. 19:7. US: The John Hopkins University Press. 1997.

http://muse.jhu.edu/journals/performing_arts_journal/summary/v019/19.1mee04.html. 29 Nov, 2011. Web.

Schmidt, Kerstin. *The Theatre of Transformation: Postmodernism in American Drama*. Rodopi B.V., 2005. Print.

Yamomo, Mele. *Defining Postmodern Theatre*. 20 May, 2007.

http://www.ezilon.com/articles/articles/5103/1/Defining-Postmodern-Theatre. 9 September, 2012. Web.

8

Trapped in Labyrinth: An Interplay of the Language of Protest through Slang and Jargon in Mahesh Dattani's *Bravely Fought the Queen* and *On a Muggy Night in Mumbai*

Rituparna Das

> ...subject is a de-centered cite where social and linguistic forces converge. (Steele, 97)

One of the notable offshoots of India's colonial encounter with the British was the aspiration to learn, read, verbally communicate and finally, write in the tongue of the masters. Repudiated, initially, the throbbing rivulet of desire, with the passage of time, gathered streams and transformed itself into a broad limitless river of Indian English writing capable of challenging the very source of it all. I can assume the image of the 'labyrinth' as an apt one for this rare type of interplay of the languages used by Mahesh Dattani in his plays to fulfill his own aim of focusing on some particular issues that beset the post-independent Indian society. It is thus, generally accepted that the absence of any particular theory in this area of language relationship where at least two languages are used simultaneously in the same context and not at all as an attitude to 'translation' other than the mode of expression, is distinctly connected to the nature of the play text itself which exists in a dialectical relationship with the performance of that same text. The labyrinthine difficulties of describing and analyzing what takes place when a play text is transposed into two languages (say, English and Hindi) simultaneously and even performed in the same way extend the problematics of describing any particular notion that works behind the expression through these languages.

Mahesh Dattani has chronicled the social victims and the follies, foibles and prejudices of Indian society. He criticizes and exposes the Indian middle class in many of his plays. To express himself Dattani studied his preference for English as he was almost obsessed to represent Indian soil and sensibility in the wake of globalization. Dattani speaks of his choice of English as his medium as one that is home-grown and Indian, a product of 'hybrid language' that is spoken normally and unobtrusively in an uninhibited way, as a matter of course by his characters who are essentially Indian. He said, "...you have got to be true to your expression also. English is for me a short of given. It's my language as it is to a lot of Indians here and abroad" (Menon and Prakash, 2003: 3). Given his chosen medium of expression, the language of his plays, as some critics have observed, obviously restricts a wider, more expansive, grass-root audience in India. That is not exactly the kind of audience that he is looking for, in every case, as he claims that his target has always been the Urban Indian upper- and middle-class audience and 'not the working class audience'. As Ann Lowry mentioned, the new English literatures are essentially a linguistic legacy of the British colonial period. The body of scholarship discussing the development of such literatures in various genres and specific regions or providing an overview of such literatures in a world context has been slowly increasing in recent years. But the research on new English literatures remains on the periphery of the traditional boundaries of English studies. When we talk about the aspects of the theatrical writing or drama, it is a bit different and also quite rare. It thus, becomes a sort of plea sometimes for the acceptance of the Indian values that are like shifting tectonic movements, where tradition and contemporary clash, 'confuse' and create a new social landscape. Dattani writes with a pungency that is skillfully disguised, employing such distinctive form of languages that resorts to clarity and sharpness, one that pushes the limits of the spoken words and the pregnant silences in between.

The supposed unnaturalness of English language as a medium of dramatic communication among the Indians has been a sore point with the Indian English dramatists. K.R. Srinivasa Iyengar refers to this when he says that the reason behind the paucity of good actable English dramas by Indians is:

> The natural medium of conversation with us...is the mother tongue rather than English, and hence, unless the characters and situations are carefully chosen, it would be difficult to make a dialogue between Indians in English sound convincing. (*Indian Writing in English*, 1995)

Dramatists who have failed to make their characters talk in English convincingly have been a victim of using the archaic English of Shakespearean heroes which will sound false, not just to an Indian ear but even to an English man. Gurucharan Das makes a valid point that the English theatre in India will have to project the kind of hybrid English we speak interspersed with Indian expressions. What Dattani says in the same context is very enlightening, "...people have to come to terms with the fact that English is an Indian Language.... India has this enormous capacity to absorb from all sources...the sooner we come to terms with that, we can get on with the rest" (*Collected Plays,* 2000). Erin Mee tells us that all Dattani's plays are first work shopped with his company Playpen in Bangalore. Dattani puts the finishing touches on his dialogues only when it is spoken aloud by actors in rehearsal. His dialogue 'is crisp and entirely functional, making for quick exchanges between characters' (Naik and Narayan, 2002: 2). The English that he uses in his plays is not the 'standard' British English, which bears an aura of imperialism and colonialism. Dattani's use of English language is based on hybridization of English words, use of Indian native words that introduce the audience to the social and cultural milieu of his plays, together with the presence of the colloquial English that most English-speaking 'post-modern' urban Indians use in everyday life. Dattani's delightful and quick repartee is an absolutely indispensable part of his style, and the wit is never lost on the audience that is comfortable with the language as well as with the milieu. Dattani says that man has created a very complex language called theatre, a language that has the ability to redefine the natural concepts of time, space and movement, a language that goes beyond the verbal and beyond the physical. Through his language of theatre, he has been able to see himself for who he is, what he has made of himself and what he aspire to be.

Now, my attempt will be to produce evidences of the way in which Mahesh Dattani though uses the medium of English to reciprocate his ideas through his plays but it has not been all to present the crude realism lying in the inner space of the high and middle-class family in the urban society. The purpose has also been served through the use of some such jargon, slang, euphemism and even the native sentence structure (the colloquial language) to mark the variety of the society itself in various strata. I shall here focus on the language of the fictional characters themselves, and the methods and contexts in which that language is conveyed. Dialogue has become of prime importance; I shall examine the spoken language of the characters encrypted in the written language of Dattani.

The play *On a Muggy Night in Mumbai* is the first of its kind elevating its prestige to the global level. Here, Dattani takes the issue of the identity of gays and lesbians. With the release of this play, the identity of Dattani has been established as a socio-radical thinker. He seems to be preoccupied with the problem-the predicament of human ambition against the expectations of social order. It is to cater the interest of urban English speaking audience in India and the audience of Indian Diaspora all over the world. Unlike other Indian English plays, this play starts with the hint of hybridism of expressions with the help of the colloquial language:

> Kamlesh: Suno.
>
> Guard: *(tucking the baton in his belt)* Ji.
>
> Kamlesh: *(takes out some more money from his wallet)* Mere kuch dost aane waale hain.
>
> Tum unko ane dena. Tum to pehchante ho sab ko.
>
> Guard: *(knowingly, after a pause)* Ji.

....

> Kamlesh: Jaldi aana.
>
> (*The guard makes to leave)*. Ek minute.
>
> (*The guard stops. Kamlesh goes to him.*) Aapki shoelace...
>
> *Kamlesh kneels before him. He is about to tie the guard's shoelace. The guard moves* away quickly.
>
> Guard: *(aghast)* yeh aap kya kar rahen hain, saab? Ji, main kar loonga.
>
> ....
>
> Kamlesh: *(rushing to him)* let me do that for you. Please....
>
> Guard: rehne do sir. Please...main kar loonga apni lace.

The level of the talking can easily be understood through the given expressions. Though a whole conversation is in Hindi, but nothing as such is described even in any footnotes. Whenever the guard appears on the stage, the same style of 'colloquialism' is followed, otherwise, throughout the play, all the characters do speak in English. There are also some uses of such words or such expressions which conventionally can be said as slang that was definitely a bold step on one hand to show the way the urban people in India talk and also, how the cosmopolitan people do use them in their own contexts at large. That can also be taken as Dattani's way of making his audience conscious of sometimes to what he tries to explain and obviously his candidness and honesty of portraying the contemporary urban society has also been reflected. While talking about the candidness, the dialogues between Sharad and Deepali in Act I, for instance, are such, which can portray again from where does Dattani is actually trying to invigorate his purpose of getting frank with the spectators about the psycho-philosophical thoughts:

> Sharad: If I had a lover, would I be such a bitch?
>
> Deepali: Don't, don't use that word. *(Clenches her fist at him)* You can call yourself a dog, call yourself a pig, but never, never insult a female.
>
> Sharad: Insult...Insult! Honey, it is with great pleasure and pride that I equate myself to a bitch!... Nobody's perfect.

....

Deepali: ... Okay, okay, you made your point.

When they argue about the orientation of 'bitch', it does makes at least the stereotypical thinking about slang into something that is obviously worth the probable meaning implied, and these sorts of explanations through the 'supposed-concocted-realistic' characters of Dattani are such that obviously not only makes this kind of portraying of dialogues also valid as a part of reason, but again, it definitely sets out as a trend in the contemporary drama structure.

Michael Walling, while commenting on the British production of *Bravely Fought the Queen*, admitted that postcolonial India and multicultural Britain both have an urgent need for a cultural expression of the contemporary human situation; they require public spaces in which the mingling of eastern and western influences takes place. This play is set around an Indian family in which the male authority is represented by two sons Jiten and Nitin, the co-partners of an advertising agency. The claustrophobic of domesticity and confined spaces are apparent through their wives Dolly and Alka, the two sisters married to the two brothers. They also have to look after their ageing mother-in-law, Ba. The play is a dramatic representation of the emptiness and shame in the lives of the cloistered women and self-indulgent unscrupulous men lost in the web of terrible secrets, deception and hypocrisy. The play aims at tearing the veil of the filthy realties and gruesome truth lie behind the presence of conservative Indian morality. Here, if we talk about the language of expressions, what occurred to me as a feature to quote is the use of 'euphemisms' on a larger prospects, which mostly defines all his methods of dramaturgy that he wants to focus on, such as, the social issues and the problems in such orthodox families that are so well covered up through some more blatant ostentatious display. Euphemism, as we all know, is used as a medium of expression which becomes a substitution of mild for the blunt expressions, as we can see in Act I of the play named, 'The Women', where almost all the conversations among the women are the part of the euphemisms implied, for instance, during the conversation where Lalitha describes the making and growing of the bonsai to Alka:

Alka: .... You must tell me how you make them.

Lalitha: What?

Alka: The bonsai.

Lalitha: Oh! The bonsai.... (*Clears her throat.*) I suppose it comes with a bit of practice. In the beginning, you will have a lot of dead shoots on your hands. But then you learn and it...comes. Anyone can do it. You first find a sapling of your choice. It could be of any tree.

....

I myself prefer fruit-bearing tree because when they are fully grown *(giggles)*—I guess you can't call them fully grown—but when they have reached their *(demonstrates with her hands)* dwarfed maturity, they really look bizarre with pea-sized mangoes and oranges!

....

Anyway, then you plant the sapling in a shallow tray—you've got to make sure the roots don't have enough space to spread. You still have to keep trimming them as they grow.

Alka: Sounds very tedious.

Lalitha: Here comes the best part...you can shape their branches into whatever shapes you want—by pinching or wiring the shoots.

Again, when Dolly and Alka are talking about Daksha, her winning of school prizes:

Dolly: *(putting the finishing touches to her make-up)* I'm sorry it has been a wasted evening for you, Lalitha. Personally, I would prefer chatting with you than bragging to strangers about how many prizes Daksha has won in school.

....

Alka: You knew. You knew and you forgot. Nitin told me you knew!

> Dolly: How could I forget such a thing? You know I was looking forward to it. We haven't been out since God knows when.
>
> Alka: *(laughs)* and you just said you would prefer talking to Lalitha than brag about Daksha's school prizes!

When Act II entitled as 'The Men' begins what have been more on focus regarding the use of expression through the language is certainly the uses of slang by them which is completely different in its defining essence when they use it. Again an expression, that was so closely indianized and for which the slang has got its stereotype, was re-structured to refurbish the language of dramaturgy. There are some uses of such slang say, 'crap', 'bastard', 'bullshit' in the dialogues of Jiten and Nitin, some so-called native slang, are also used when Jiten is scolding Sridhar at one point or addressing him out of anger. Sometimes these expressions can also be treated as jargons in a way when they are barbarous or debased language, but not though gibberish.

Some other points quite worthy to be noted regarding Dattani's use of expressions in the language are—the differences and the contradictions—which can be explained as the types of his expressions though, may be small, but still distinctive points like, the uses of slang in both the plays, moving in different motifs, and also the words chosen for expressing Ba in *Bravely Fought the Queen*, where it is visualized that Dattani has not used any sort of Indian words or even native expressions of language, when at the same time we understood the way she is talking, her position of conversation and some of her orthodox traits; whereas, we see the independent use of such colloquial words in *On a Muggy Night in Mumbai* as I mentioned before to put the distinctions among the characters residing as a part of urban Indian society. They are not even italicized. John McRae said in his 'A Note on the Play' of *On a Muggy Night in Mumbai* that these changes are a part of 'refinement' and 'development' of Dattani's writing as well as his dramatic techniques.

Hence, after my above discussions, I want to state about such interplays of the forms and expressions of language which are employed so well to make Mahesh Dattani a new and unconventional voice in Indian theatre. No doubt, a new trend has been set through this. The echo of his theatrical art both in terms of form and content, anticipate his prominence in the theatrical world at global level. The flexibility and ease of expressions, breaking the barriers of tight-fisted dramaturgy would add a new dimension to the edge of theatrical canon.

Works Cited

Agrawal, B.R. and M.P. Sinha. *Major Trends in the Post-Independence Indian English Fiction.* New Delhi: Atlantic Publishers and Distributors, 2003. Print.

Agarwal, Malti. (ed.). *New Perspectives on Indian English Writings.* New Delhi: Atlantic Publishers and Distributors, 2007. Print.

Biswas, Sarbojit and Arindam Das (eds.). *Colonial Spectre and Beyond: Studies in Indian Writing in English.* Kolkata: Books Way, 2011. Print.

Dattani, Mahesh. *Collected Plays.* New Delhi: Penguin Books India, 2000. Print.

Iyengar, K.R. Srinivasa. *Indian Writing in English.* New Delhi: Sterling, 1985. Print.

Latha, A. Madhavi. "Dattani's Dramatic Technique" in *Multicultural Theatre and Drama.* (Ed.) T. Sai Chandra Mouli. New Delhi: Authors Press, 2011. Print.

Lowry, Ann. "Style Range in New English Literatures" in *The Other Tongue: English Across Cultures.* (Ed.) Braj B. Kachru. New Delhi: Oxford University Press, 1996. Print.

McRae, John. A Note on the Play *On a Muggy Night in Mumbai. Collected Plays.* By Mahesh Dattani. New Delhi: Penguin Books India, 2000. Print.

Menon, Rajiv and K.S. Prakash. "Theatre to Morning Raga". *The Hindu,* Hyderabad 02 July, 2003. Print.

Naik, M.K. "The Achievement of Indian Drama in English". *Perspectives on Indian Drama in English.* (Ed.) M.K. Naik and S. Mokashi Punekar. Madras: Oxford University Press, 1977. Print.

Naik, M.K. and Shyamala A. Narayan. *Indian English Literature: 1980-2000—A Critical Survey.* New Delhi: Sterling Publishers, 2002. Print.

Steele, Meili. *Theorizing Textual Subjects: Agency and Oppression.* Cambridge: Cambridge University Press, 1997. Print.

Walling, Michael. "A Note on the Play *Bravely Fought the Queen*". *Collected Plays.* By Mahesh Dattani. New Delhi: Penguin Books India, 2000. Print.

9

Mahesh Dattani's Plays on Music and Dance: A Reading of *Morning Raga* and *Dance Like a Man*

Tuhin Majumdar and *Nandini Maity*

Mahesh Dattani in his plays deals with the cultural contexts in such a way that several revelations or hidden truths can be brought out through the deliberate silences or sub-text in his plays which sometimes possess the disruptive power to crumble the entire foundation of the society. The two plays, under discussion, *Morning Raga* and *Dance Like a Man* not only enliven the past through Carnatic music and the ancient dance form *Bharatanatyam*, but also foreground the present Indian cultural problems of identity and stereotyped gender roles. These two plays form a rich compendium of dialogues, songs and dance, interspersed throughout the plays. Dattani pays a tribute to India's rich cultural heritage and also to the artists and some of the nationalist leaders who risked their reputations in order to revive these forms of classical arts which not only resists to some extent the overtly commercialized influence of Western culture but also alleviates our spirits and brings about a perfect harmony between our body and soul.

One of the largest, most populous and certainly most culturally diverse countries of the world—the spectrum of India's cultural fabric is decidedly complex and difficult to encompass. Therefore, when we talk about Indian theatre, we enter a vast and intricate arena which is heterogeneous and polyglot in character. The theatres are extraordinarily inclusive. It encompasses the classical dance forms like the *Kathakali* or *Bharatanatyam*, the rituals such as *Raas* or the *Ramlila*, the folk forms like *Jatra* in Bengal, *Nautanki* of Uttar Pradesh, *Tamasha* of Maharastra and *Bhavai* of Gujarat. Even the modern devices like Epic theatre sometimes bewilderingly intermingle with indigenous theatrical elements. Dance, music, instrumentation, drama all combine together happily in a theatre performed by an array of artists working simultaneously.

With the arrival of the Indian dramatists like Mahesh Dattani in the 1980s the audiences began to feel more at home. With the multiple varieties of Indian English that is internalized and spoken without premeditation, Indian theatre in English began to emerge with a distinctive and vigorous identity. Dattani is a modern Indian English playwright who has successfully staged his plays in India and abroad. He finds a significant position among some notable playwrights and directors such as Badal Sircar, Vijay Tendulkar, Girish Karnad, etc. who have contributed much to the growth and development of Indian theatre. Most of these playwrights uphold various strands of Indian culture in their works.

Dattani is an actor, director and interestingly trained in Western Ballet under Molly Andre at Alliance Françoise de Bangalore (1984-87) and *Bharatanatyam* under Chandrabhaga Devi and Krishna Rao, Bangalore (1986-90). He formed his own theatre group, 'Playpen' in 1984. He possesses an innate sense of dialogues that is lucid, stimulating and effective both for the actors as well as the audiences. Dealing with the compelling issues deeply rooted in his milieu, he has dispelled the perception about English theatre being just a gratuitous fizz. His audiences have been large and responsive, both to the spectacle and the dialogues. In his book, *Form and Meaning in Mahesh Dattani's Plays*, Prof. Bijay Kumar Das has divided Dattani's plays into six broad categories:

1. Plays on Violence and Crime (*Seven Steps Around the Fire, The Swami and Winston, Uma and Fairy Queen* and *Final Solutions*)

2. Plays on Gay and Lesbian relationship (*On a Muggy Night in Mumbai, Mango Soufflé, Do the Needful* and here we can also include *Seven Steps Around the Fire*)
3. Plays on Natural Calamities (*Clearing the Rubble* and *The Tale of a Mother Feeding Her Child*)
4. Family Plays (*Thirty Days in September, Bravely Fought the Queen, Where's a Will* and here we can include *Do the Needful)*
5. Plays on Music and Dance (*Morning Raga* and *Dance Like a Man*)
6. Plays on Disease and Disabled (*Ek Alag Mausam* and *Tara*). (Das 163)

In this paper, we have mainly focused on the fifth category, that is, the Plays on Music and Dance and showed how Dattani, through his two plays, *Morning Raga* and *Dance Like a Man* tries to uphold Indian culture and tradition through the ancient art forms of *Carnatic* music and the classical dance form, *Bharatanatyam.*

Carnatic Music is the nucleus from which Dattani's play-or more accurately-screenplay *Morning Raga* is born. It is written and directed by Dattani with an ensemble cast including subtle actors like Shabana Azmi and Perizaad Zorabian. Hitting the Indian silver screens on 29th October, 2004, the international premier of the film was a part of the Cairo Film Festival in December 2004. *Carnatic* Music belongs to the southern part of Indian subcontinent. A sub-genre of Indian classical music, *Carnatic* Music stems from ancient Hindu tradition and mythology and differs from Hindustani Music which is imbued with Persian and Islamic influences.

Set in the locale of Andhra Pradesh countryside, the story moves to and fro between binary extremes—the supersonic Hyderabad and a serene village of South India. When the city musicians are busy making money from trash jingles aping Western music, in the village women devote their entire life as students of *Carnatic* Music with no materialistic aspirations. Dattani attempts to create a confluence of these two worlds.

While explaining the screenplay in a telephonic conversation with Shabana Azmi, he claims:

> The play is about meeting of two worlds. A story that brings together the modern and the traditional unites the past with the present, *Carnatic* music with Western music, fate and coincidences with individual choices. ("A Note on the Play", Shabana Azmi)

The music of audience's applause is what every musician desires. Swarnalatha, the protagonist, is no exception. Her only dream is to sing *Carnatic* Music in front of a big audience at some concerts in the city. However, little did she know that her coveted dream would turn out to be a nightmare of trauma and guilt. Swarnalatha shares an inextricable bond of sisterhood and friendship with Vaishnavi who accompanies her in playing violin. She is her complement. Music binds them together. Vaishnavi's husband disliked her playing the violin. However, Swarnalatha's repeated request persuaded the reluctant Vaishnavi to join her for the city concert.

Tragedy strikes. The bus meets with an accident while crossing the bridge. Colliding with a car, the bus falls into the river. Vaishnavi and Swarnalatha's son are killed. This fateful incident wrecked Swarnalatha's mental poise. Shell-shocked, she chooses a self-imposed exile. She swears never to sing again or cross the bridge to the city. She assumes that God has punished her for her soaring ambitions. She almost becomes a patient of 'Posttraumatic Stress Disorder' (PTSD) which usually generate from life threatening traumas like assault, natural disaster, accident or torture. Indifferent to her art, she hides in her private cocoon and gets solace in performing domestic chores.

Time flies by. Twenty years hence, Vaishnavi's son Abhinay—who has music in his DNA—decides to pursue his mother's vocation of composing music. Tired of composing 'stuffs' like jingles, he quits the lucrative job of composing for advertisements. He decides to start a music troupe to compose everlasting music like the time immemorial Charminar, a monument and mosque in Hyderabad built by Muhammad Quli Qutub Shah to commemorate the eradication of plague.

Abhinay visits his native village after a span of twenty years on the day of the death anniversary of his mother Vaishnavi. He spots Swarnalatha, enquires her about his mother and follows her as she turns a deaf ear to his queries. They reach the accursed bridge which changed Swarnalatha's life twenty years before. Just then, coincidentally, a car being driven by a city-bred girl called Pinkie comes and hits Abhinay. He escapes major injury. The guilt of being the cause of the bus accident which took away her friend and son twenty years before is suddenly triggered. Swarnalatha screams.

The severe effect of trauma on a person can be observed in his/her avoidance of people, places and events closely or roughly associated with the traumatic incident. In Swarnalatha's case, it was the bridge that instead of connecting talent with success, subtracted two important persons from her life. And reworking of similar accident, the moment she steps on the bridge triggers her arousal symptoms of panic.

Pinkie's car required repairing. She is compelled to be a guest in Abhinay's house for the night-stay. They both shares interest in music. Pinkie offers to sing in his band. They accelerated towards Hyderabad for the talent-hunt to form the proposed troop. Thanks to the business connections of Pinkie's mother, the enterprising Mrs. Kapoor who was instrumental in arranging the first show for their band in a restaurant. The name of their band "Pratibimb" is soaked with symbolic connotations. A Hindi word, it means reflection. It is the reflection of the tragic past which haunts Swarnalatha. The faint reflections of his mother playing the violin, drives Abhinay to pursue the rough road to form a band. Pinkie too has her share of blurred reflection of her father whose death is still shrouded in mystery. However, their maiden performance could neither impress the foodie-audience in the restaurant nor its Manager. When asked for an honest opinion about their music, the Manager was blatantly frank, "There are hundreds, thousands of young musicians in this city and they all think they are different or unique, but they are not... you are one of them" (Dattani, *Morning Raga*).

In the meantime, Mrs. Kapoor lays bare the secret to Pinkie that her drunkard father was responsible for the bus accident in the bridge as he was driving under the influence of alcohol. Pinkie tries, but fails to tell this to Abhinay. Heart broken by the band's performance, Abhinay drinks. However, in the morning he gets a courier from Swarnalatha containing his mother's violin, which she had treasured so long. He comes to her house to express his gratitude. Swarnalatha assumes that he may blame her for his misfortunes. On the contrary, he requests her to lend her voice for his band. As expected, Swarnalatha declines. The reason is obvious. Her husband too insists her to sing. Abhinay reminds her of the past and tries to convince her emotionally:

> Because it's me who is asking Vaishnavi's son. My mother played for you. You can sing for me. Or you don't want to return the favour because she is dead and it does not matter anymore? (Dattani, *Morning Raga*)

Abhinay's father, who wants his son to look after his ancestral lands, gets irked with Swarnalatha. He asks her, "Please leave him alone. Music will take him nowhere". She is enraged at this slur to *Carnatic* music. She does not respond to him as it would be meaningless to argue about musical art with a person who understands only agriculture. She turns to Abhinay and says, "I will sing for you". Next morning, she with her husband starts for the city-concert. Unfortunately, their car breaks down. They are forced to take the bus which crosses the bridge. Just when the bus mounts the bridge, she starts screaming, stops the bus, runs back to the village and falls ill. The concert and her attempt to come to terms with the past fails.

Next day, she calls up Pinkie, apologizes and promises to teach her *Carnatic* music so that she can sing for the band. After a rigorous training, Pinkie is all set to perform the *Sindu Bhairavi* or the Morning Raga, which was Vaishnavi's favourite. As the day of the concert approached, Pinkie decides to unravel the truth. In a desperate effort, she speeds up the car towards the bridge when Swarnalatha was in the front seat to prove that she was not cursed. The tension was so thick that it could have been sliced with a knife:

> Pinkie—I hope you will find it in you to forgive me.
>
> Pinkie puts her car in top gear and speeds towards the bridge.

> *Swarnalatha realizes that she is going over the bridge. Her panic attack starts.*
>
> Swarnalatha—No! Please! Stop the car!
>
> Pinkie—I just want to show you that it is not your fault!
>
> Abhinay—What are you doing?
>
> Pinkie—To show you that there is no curse on you!
>
> *Swarnalatha holds on to Pinkie to prevent her from driving further*
>
> Swarnalatha—Stop it! Stop the car! We will all die.
>
> Abhinay—(*holding Swarnalatha back*)
>
> Calm down! Stop the car! *Swarnalatha.*
>
> (Dattani. *Morning Raga*. 22 April, 2014 Web)

Pinkie stops the car in the middle of the bridge. Nothing happens. There is a stoic calm in the air. Pinkie breaks down in tears. She confesses that it was her drunkard father who should be held responsible for the accident and if Swarnalatha cannot forgive him then at least she should no more blame herself for the accident. The guilt in Swarnalatha's subconscious that has made her nervous all those twenty years is now drained off. Eventually, she comes to the city-concert and on repeated urging from Pinkie, she sings *Thaa ye Yashoda*. Before singing the song she addresses the audience:

> It has been my dream to sing for the audience such as you. But tonight, I will sing this song for my son, who like my music has returned after a very long journey. Abhinay, I sing this raga for you—my son. (Dattani, *Morning Raga*, 2014)

So long Swarnalatha grieves her friend Vaishnavi's death more than the loss of her only son. Now, she openly accepts Abhinay as her son. The wheel of fate has turned a full circle and the play ends with wish fulfillment for Abhinay and Swarnalatha. The song *Thaa ye Yashoda* is so apt to describe this newly discovered mother-son relationship. Attuned to the Hindu mythology, the lyrics of the song exemplify the acts of mischief of young Lord Krishna. The young Krishna who is the supreme Lord is also the cynosure of the *gopis* (a Sanskrit word which refers to group of cow herding girls—mentioned in Vaishnava Theology—who had unconditional devotion and love towards Lord Krishna) who complains to his mother Yashoda about his son's mischievous acts. The classical song is fused not only with English lyrics "O Yashoda the son of your's/ There is none like him in the Universe" (Dattani, *Morning Raga*, *Torbox.net*), but also arranged with accompaniments like keyboard, electric guitar and drums which usually goes with Western music. This symbiotic blending of the two worlds, ideologies, institutions and generations or the gelling of past and present make *Morning Raga* an emotionally gripping story with psycho-analytical depths.

Indeed, in treatment of trauma singing is instrumental. It is a neuromuscular activity which helps in releasing blockages of energy as traumatized people gets frozen. The act of singing is nourishing. One can sense the life force, one's ability to create. To own one's voice is to own one's authority over oneself and thereby ending the subjugation of trauma and dominating elements of victimization. Dattani's play *Morning Raga,* which deals with music and its therapeutic effect, gives him the requisite dynamic force as a playwright and adds variety to his writing faculty.

Dattani is among the few writers to perceive the continued violence of the postcolonial nationalists' discourses and propose the idea of an all-inclusive democracy to come. In his play *Dance Like a Man*, Dattani upholds and thereby deconstructs the idea of Indianness by arguing the case of those citizens of India who doesn't belong to the mainstream professional *Bharatanatyam* dancers, a dance form, which was marginalized in the post-independence India owing to its origin (a dance form of the Temple dancers). *Dance Like a Man* is such a text in which local color predominates, as the play revolves round the daily activities of a particular South-Indian family, and thus, becoming an important subtext. The cultural ambience of a *Bharatanatyam* household, the gaudy sarees, the sounds in the background often recognized as *Carnatic* background music together build up an intense sense of a cultural space that is integral to the shaping of individual characters in the play. Dattani, in *Dance Like a Man*, explores as well as juxtaposes the contemporary and early history of India in strictly personal terms and the play also probes into conflict of the three generations. Pitted against the background of classical dance form, *Bharatanatyam* and *Carnatic* music and drawing upon centuries—old traditions, to stage a play in English is hardly a mean achievement.

The age old ritualistic tradition of paying homage to gods and goddesses through dance and music has permeated Indian life and has become an essential feature of Indian culture. In the colonial period it was and even in the present it is still believed that the classical dance and music mirrors traditional India's rich cultural heritage. Since the historical periods India has a tradition of music and dance. *Carnatic* and *Hindustani* music which has a historical continuity of thousands of years are the two most important styles of classical music in India. These classical music forms are the soul of all the art forms in India as they not only manifest India's cultural heritage but are also spiritually alleviating.

A wide variety of classical dances in India started as temple dances. Later as they became an integral part of theatres, these dance forms were modified to a large extent and became very much acceptable in the society. *Bharatanatyam* is the most renowned dance form of Tamil Nadu in particular and South India in general. It was originally performed by the temple dancers, *Devadasis*. Lord Shiva is treated as the God of this dance form. Bharat Muni, the pole star of Indian aesthetics in his monumental work *Natyashastra,* a compendium of performing arts discusses the dance form of *Bharatanatyam*. With its quintessential grace and sculpturesque postures, this dance form had been kept alive by the efforts and struggles of the Gurus and their disciples.

Now let us trace the socio-political history of this ancient dance form, *Bharatanatyam*. The revival of a very old dance form (originally known as *Sadri* and was performed in the court of the Chola Rajas), was actually a nationalist endeavor of the Congress activists like Rukmini Devi, E. Krishna Iyer and Annie

Besant who tried hard to detach the dance from its disreputable history associated with the temple dancers, the *Devdasis* and thereby trace its source in the works of Bharat Muni. The two ancient theoretical works on classical dance forms (*Natyashastra*) and acting (*Abhinaya Darpana*), written probably around second or third century B.C. are generally ascribed to Bharat Muni. For this reason the name is *Bharatanatyam* or the dance form codified by Bharat Muni. The revival of this dance form, *Bharatanatyam* (also connotes 'Bharatiya' or Indian dance) was also an act of cultural revival and postcolonial nationalist resistance against Western dances. It was a kind of cultural protest against the colonizers by showing them that we, the Indians, though colonized, are not at all savages; on the contrary, possess a rich cultural heritage. After the independence, the dance form became an important way to uphold India's rich cultural heritage in the West. In Dattani's play, *Dance Like a Man,* Jairaj, Ratna and especially Lata's dance help to transform them into cultural icons of the nation. The packaging of the erotic dance *ashtapadi* into a carefully researched cultural artifact transforms Lata from a simple dancing girl, pleasure to audiences' eyes, into national cultural icon, a cultural diva.

In Indian classical dance forms, music and drama are closely interlinked. In order to represent this trend and culture and do proper justice with them, Dattani gives dance and music a pivotal role in his plays. Dance is the main issue that has been raised in the plays as *Bravely Fought the Queen* and *Dance Like a Man*.

Dance Like a Man is a very popular and highly acclaimed play providing a deep insight into the contemporary Indian social scenario. "The universality of its theme and the quality of Dattani's script has made it something of a cultural flagship for contemporary Indian theatre" (qtd. in Sen n.p.). The play features Jairaj, the male protagonist and his wife, Ratna engaged in taking training in classical dance, *Bharatanatyam* which is intolerable to Amritlal, father of Jairaj. Dattani is very well acquainted with the middle-class society which considers dance as strictly meant for women. He exploits this notion fully to his advantage in the portrayal of the patriarchal culture. The play *Dance Like a Man* is akin to the traditional Indian folk theatres in its minimalistic stage design. Dattani, through his play, revives one of the oldest dance form in modern Indian theatre, reminding both the audience and the readers of our cultural roots and showing in the process how heredity and society both condition an individual's life.

Dattani, apart from dealing with the themes like communal violence, crime, homo-eroticism, the breaking down of joint family system, also deals with the finer aesthetic aspects such as dance and music. In *Dance Like a Man*, Dattani delves deep into the heart of the classical dancers, artists and singers who seek recognition. Dance and music provides aesthetic pleasure and transcend the basic instinct of human beings and bring joy to their minds. But the biggest irony is that some people belonging to the orthodox Hindu society like that of Amritlal in the play *Dance Like a Man* abhors and is opposed to dance. But their children are strongly determined and cultivate the art of *Bharatanatyam* against all odds. The reviews on Lata's dance speak volumes for the sublime aspect of dance. It goes like this:

> Her rendition of the *ashtapad* from *Geeta Govinda* was tenderly intense and intensely tender. The audience was transported to Gokulam and witnessed Radha pining for a divine lover, who has failed to arrive. Lata's tearful expression and heaving bosom conveyed all that was humanly possible. (Dattani, 2006: 58)

The passion for dance and the love for music are depicted through the protagonists of this play. Dattani shows that the fulfillment in the life of these characters in the play comes through their success in dance and music. On being asked why *Dance Like a Man* ends with Ratna's voice saying, "then we had all the grace, all the brilliance, all the magic to dance like gods", and what she meant by "dance like gods", Dattani answered, "Dance with perfection. In traditional dance, only Shiv is the perfect dancer" (Das, 2008: 163).

Dattani began his career chiefly as a dramatist and he also wrote for the radio as well as for the films. As these genres are performative in nature, it is quite natural that music and dance forms an integral part of these genres. Most of Dattani's plays incorporate several genres. In his play *Dance Like a Man*—which was later made into a film by Pamela Rooks in 2003, released in 2005, and won a National Film Award for the Best Feature Film in English—he integrates dance and music as indispensible part of the story line. Dattani himself is a trained *Bharatanatyam* dancer and this fact has a vital influence on this play. In the playwright's note on this play, *Dance Like a Man* Dattani describes this particular dance form as a "fascinating history of oppression and renaissance" as well as the way in which it is being commodified in the present India in order to sell in the West.

Dattani, both in the play and in his note, is critical of the endeavors of elite Indians, especially the "comprador bourgeois" who sanitized these dance forms, cleansing them of their erotic moves, divorcing them from their history, that is, the history of the temple dancers, the *Devadasi*s, persecuting the *Devadasi*s who actually created this dance forms and performed them, and commodifying them for export. The *Devadasi*, also known as the temple dancers traditionally worshipped Shiva in the role of Nataraja, the lord of all dance forms. But as a result of the subsequent decay of Hindu culture due to the advent of the British administrators there was a transition of the *Devadasi*s to prostitutes. Through this play, *Dance Like a Man*, Dattani tries to explore the colonial and postcolonial nationalist biases against these conventional dance forms that make the postcolonial elite and a patriarch Amritlal insist his daughter-in-law, Ratna to stop going to dance classes to take dance lessons from an aged, almost dying *Devadasi*, the only living exponent in the Mysore school of classical dance. Thus, Amritlal becomes instrumental in the death of this age old tradition and for Ratna being only a mediocre dancer. Due to the lack of a good tutor, Ratna fails to achieve the absolute perfection of this particular dance form which seeks the aesthetic blending of both spirituality as well as eroticism and only becomes successful to be a little more than a thing of pleasure to the audience. Amritlal also strictly opposes the Indian tradition of male dancing that his only son, Jairaj wants to learn. As Chambers points out:

> Certain regions, such as Tanjore, now in Tamil Nadu, and parts of Andhra Pradesh, have their own dance dramas.

> Bhagawat Mela Natak and Kutchipudi respectively, in which until recently all parts, including female ones were played by men. Yet cross-gender roles were also imposed by necessity, because the stigma against *Devadasis* in the early 20th century meant that few respectable women could be found to perform the dance. The early pioneer of the *Bharatanatyam* revival, E. Krishna Iyer, dressed as a woman to promote the dance form and encourage women to perform the dance on the stage.

Dance Like a Man chiefly focuses on Indian classical dance which signifies the art forms commonly found in much of Dattani's works. The classical music and dances in India suffered from various colonial prejudices and also the prudery of the postcolonial Indian elites. Dattani, through his plays, gives due honor to India's rich classical legacy and to the middle-class exponents of these dance forms who are willing to leave no stone unturned by keeping these art forms alive within people inside and outside India. *Dance Like a Man*, is in many ways inspired by "a few young dancers from 'respectable' families [who] shocked the public by learning the dance from the *Devadasis*.... It is to the credit of the enthusiasts who fought society that we are today still linked with this grand classical art form" (Dattani, Playwright's Note, 107). Dattani's attempts at voicing the historic pre-colonial classical art forms through a postcolonial play are significant for various reasons. It strengthens and fortifies the connection between sensuous, aesthetic and spiritual which is typical to these traditional art forms but which has often been looked down upon or stamped out in colonial as well as the postcolonial India. It also makes the best use of these classical art forms to provide a transgressive space that both criticizes middle-class morality of the Indians and also tries to provide an unorthodox way of living peacefully in the world.

Dattani shows that in *Dance Like a Man* there are numerous references to Lord Shiva or the Nataraja, who transgresses all the fixed gender roles. As observed by Uma Narayan, every *Bharatanatyam* dancer is well aware of the legend of Shiva and Shakti as the legendary *Ardhanarishawari*—combination of the dance of the eternal *Purush* (man) and *Prakriti* (woman). In this play Jairaj and Ratna begins to learn the divine dance of lord Shiva and Parvati and they are so moved by it that they even name their son, Shankara, another name of Lord Shiva. When Ratna's performance of *Bharatanatyam* wins admiration from the viewers, the hetero-normative cultural values are strengthened once again.

Later in the play we find Ratna trying to fulfill her long cherished dreams through her daughter, Lata by spending time to uphold India's cultural tradition for not only national but also international audiences and persuading Dr. Gowda taking Lata in his group of performers for the renowned festival of India to be held in Canada. We cannot deny the fact that although Lata can see clearly through the pretense of her audience and also her critics, her mother Ratna continues the commodification of this dance form instead of protecting its dignity and integrity; she spends all her time in packaging India's cultural traditions for the audiences worldwide. People often ask question: How long will it be before India, already sucked into the vortex of globalization loses its core cultural identity? In our endeavor to create in the world outside an awareness of India and its 'Indianness', it seems that we Indians have embarked on festivals and cultural diplomatic missions, packaging culture and exporting it.

It is also true that no nation can afford to cling to its past because changes in ideas and styles are inevitable with the progress of time. Tradition, as one believes, is not as orthodox as one imagines, nor is modernity as radical as one fear. Our cultural identities are essentially built on differences in lifestyle emphasis. Ideas are universal, but born in specific contexts. What Dattani wants to point out is that as long as culture remains rooted to what are its essential truths, it can acquire temporarily and then discard in its passage through time what is adventitious. As long as our arts remain internalized journeys of the subliminal stages of consciousness, unrelated to changes in and around us, no force can destroy our music and dance, which is its outward visual dimension.

When Vishwas, Lata's fiancée voices his conservative attitude about the erotic dance *ashtapadi* that Lata usually performs, Jairaj immediately points out that Ratna, his wife used to perform *ashtapadi* thirty years ago. Vishwas is perplexed but admires Ratna's guts in performing such a sensuous movement as *ashtapadi* that stands as a contrast and clearly contradicts the postcolonial middle-class ideas of feminity and also Jairaj's liberal frame of mind in allowing his wife to dance this particular move, but it is also quite clear that if he is provided with a choice he would never allow his wife perform this particular movement.

At the far end of the play, the protagonist, Jairaj's house is pulled down and he and his wife shift to "a posh flat" for living peacefully for the remaining a few years of their life. Despite her promise to her parents, there is no hint that Lata will still continue to dance in future that her parents wanted her to and loved so much. Putting aside these negatives, Dattani ends the play with a vision of the young Ratna and Jairaj in a perfectly happy state laughing and preparing themselves to dance together. As he visualizes his dead wife slowly move towards him, the now—dead Jairaj says:

> We dance perfectly. In unison. Not missing a step or a beat. We talk and laugh at all the mistakes we made in our previous dances.... We are only human. We lacked the brilliance. We lacked the magic to dance like God. (Dattani. *Dance Like a Man*, 2006: 74)

Though, it is a very potent vision, yet it is clear that it can only be fulfilled through death and also suggests how the playwright feels about the hazards that still continue to bother the Indian dancers even today. The final performance of Jairaj and Ratna reinforces the promise of spirituality embodied in the *Devadasi* tradition of *Bharatanatyam* but does not eradicate or at least neutralize the hurdles and challenges endemic to this tradition. Dattani comments:

> I would like to challenge the assumption of what is Indian. Does that mean traditional theatre forms? Yes, they're wonderful, they're very sophisticated, they're impressive, but are they really India? That's something I would like to question and challenge. And they really reflecting life as it is now, that is the question I would like to ask. They're fine but there is the danger that

> if you look at them as if they are quintessential India you're doing those forms a great disservice, because you are not allowing them to change. What we need to do now is to look at those forms and say we're approaching the twenty-first century, this is who we are and this is our legacy, so where do we take that. (qtd. in Sen n.p)

By scrutinizing the different classical art forms from a historical perspective, it is very much evident that Mahesh Dattani, through his plays especially *Morning Raga* and *Dance Like a Man* upholds the true spirit of the quintessential India, voices his resistance against the continuous cultural dominance by the West and brings the marginalized art forms into the mainstream culture opening the eyes of the readers to their rich cultural legacy.

Works Cited

Bhattacharya, Nandini. "The Guide: Colonial Encounters and Postcolonial Transformations". *R.K. Narayan's The Guide: New Critical Perspectives*. Delhi: Worldview Publications, 2004. 86-87. Print.

Chaudhuri, Asha Kuthari. *Mahesh Dattani: An Introduction*. Delhi: Foundation Books, 2005. Print.

Das, Bijay Kumar. *Form and Meaning in Mahesh Dattani's Plays*. New Delhi: Atlantic Publishers & Distributors, 2008. Print.

Dattani, Mahesh. *Dance Like a Man: A Stage Play in Two Acts*. New Delhi: Penguin Books, 2006. Print.

——. *Morning Raga: A Screen Play*. "A Note on the Play" Google Books: Penguin. 22 Apr. 2014. Web.

——. *Morning Raga*. Dir. Mahesh Dattani. Perf. Shabana Azmi, Perizaad Zorabian, Prakash Kovelamudi, Lillete Dubey. R K Teleshow, 2004. Film.

Orth, Jaap. "Music Therapy with Traumatized Refugees in a Clinical Setting." *Voices: A World Forum for Music Therapy*, 5.2 (2005): (n.p). 22 Apr. 2014. Web.

Sen, Asha. "Looking Back, Looking Forward: Examining Pre-Colonial Identities in Mahesh Dattani's *Dance Like a Man.*" *Ariel: A Review of International English Literature*, 42.2 (2011): 129-47. 22 Apr. 2014. Web.

10

Rethinking Gender: A Critical Study of Dattani's *Do the Needful*

Ayesha Anwar Warsi

Gender, one of the most debated terms in the English Language, has always been a burning subject. In the contemporary critical scenario, it is a much contested and intensely complicated concept. Gender Studies, being a vastly expanding subject, is conceived of all cultural and historical aspects that talks about gender roles, alternative sexuality and gender identity with regard to societal space David Glover and Kora Kaplan in the "Introduction" to their book *Genders: The New Critical Idiom* have said:

> According to Dr. Samuel Johnson's *A Dictionary of English Language* (1785), gender could refer either to the grammatical practice of classifying nouns as masculine, feminine or neuter; or it could mean 'a sex'.... Gender continues to function as a grammatical term, for example, as well as being a euphemism for a person's sex, though it is no longer used as a synonym for sexual act. (Glover and Kaplan. *Genders: The New Critical Idiom,* XI 2007)

The word gender, thus, has always created uneasiness in an attempt to differentiate between sex and gender. No other branch of study but feminism has critically observed both the terms and found that, "sex is biological while gender is socially constructed" (Judith Butler, 1990) of social construction which implies that a "sexed body" undergoes an "imposed social category". This imposed social category has given birth to innumerable reactionary discourses stemming from the history of the politics of exclusion which these socially constructed categories have faced for ages. The reactionary discourses, however, not only mean gender studies but they cover a broader spectrum categorically falling under cultural studies; including all readings which relate to our culture whether it be Feminism or Feminisms, Postcolonialism, Lesbian and Gay criticism, Dalit writings or any other Deconstructive reading. The intellectual labour has necessiated reading against the grain such that dominant heterosexuality where society like ours locating gender within the circumference of our culture has become a challenging issue. Berthold Schoene, in his paper "Queer Politics, Queer Theory, and the Future of Identity" published in an anthology entitled *A Cambridge Companion to Feminist Literary Theory* edited by Ellen Rooney, argues:

> The new Queer identity, projected by critics such as Thomas and Tatchell, emerged from the utopian fantasy of a perfect reassemblage of our original sexual "self-and-otherness," or hetero/homo/hybridity, which we have come to unlearn under hetero-normative pressures. (Schoene, 295)

Therefore, challenging characteristics of the patriarchal and the heterosexual social set up has urged writers to use "literature as an instrument of liberation". In this literature the writers bring to the fore what was often lost or most of the times was overshadowed by the traditional pillar which the society is built on. Particularly, largely missing in these discourses of actions are the invisible issues which the society predominantly comprises of. It becomes, thus, almost impossible to assign a singular or proper identity to these sociological reductions. However, our writers have an active relation to these hidden issues and through their writings they have recognized the unwillingness of the threatened identities of these genders. Amongst the Indian playwrights Mahesh Dattani occupies a privileged place in driving these hidden issues to the platform where they could be apparently visible.

Mahesh Dattani, a Bangalore born graduate in History, Economics, and Political Science, and a postgraduate in Marketing and Advertising Management, is a copywriter, a full time theatre professional, is also a film director who made his debut with the film *Mango Soufflé*. *Morning Raga* is another film which he wrote and directed. As a playwright his major plays include—*Where There's a Will* (1988), *Dance Like a Man* (1989), *Tara* (1990), *Bravely Fought the Queen* (1991), *Final Solutions* (1993), *On a Muggy Night in Mumbai* (1998), *Seven Steps Around the Fire* (a radio play for BBC, 1998), etc. and out of these, *Dance Like a Man* was featured as a film which, by the National panorama in 1998, was awarded as the "Best Picture in English". *Final Solutions* won him the Sahitya Akademi Award, and in 1997 Sahitya Kala Parishad chose *Final Solutions* as the best production of the year including *Tara* and *Thirty Days in September* (2007). Although academically unlinked with Drama and theatre, Dattani had always been passionate for theatrical art. He emerged as one of the most splendid playwrights in the tradition of Indian English Drama. His primary aim was always to manifest the cause of the underprivileged segments of society. Beena Agarwal, in her book, *Mahesh Dattani's Plays: A New Horizon in Indian Theatre*, has said about him:

> He prepared the stage for a specific realism on the lines of Ibsen and Shaw. For him man is an integral part of society and consciously and unconsciously the creeping influence of societal set up, determine the fabric of relationship around him. (Agarwal, 2008: 25)

Experimenting with human nature, through his theatrical and dramatic skills, Dattani has wonderfully surfaced the modern urban evil of sex perverts (the alternative sexuality, even when regarded as unsocial, now illegal but not illogical and unnatural at all, fulfills biological need of the man and escapes him from repression) of Indian society like homosexuality, child abuse, communal disharmony, problems relating to gender, restrictions imposed by the phallocentric world, the question of identity, etc. He, the most successful of the Indian playwrights is among those who have drawn their substance from the changing trends and the contemporary climate including the socio-cultural situation of the time. According to a Sahitya akademi award citation, on the back cover of Dattani's book, *Collected Plays,* "Dattani's work probes tangled attitudes in contemporary India towards communal differences, consumerism and gender...a brilliant contribution to Indian drama in English." He has particularly brought in light, in most of his plays, the invisible issue of homosexuality, which occupies a gendered place in society, "while still focusing on human relationships and personal and moral choices which are the classic concern of world drama" (Dattani, 2000). David Glover and Cora Kaplan in their book *Genders: The New Critical Idiom,* while talking of Djuna Barnes' 1936 novel *Nightwood,* have confirmed that:

> Both modernism and same sex passion have relied upon the twentieth-century metropolis as a place sufficiently large and diverse to enable them to survive, and eventually to flourish. (Glover and Kaplan, 2007: 112)

The playwright has, thus, brought to the fore a changing attitude of metropolitan social set up which is based on repression of the sexual desire by legalizing the truly vague context of the right to self determination that one admits to one's existence. The subject matter he has taken to portray is tabooed, unsocial, illegal, abnormal but not unnatural and unbiological for human existence. His characters are based on an existentialist ethics which defines it as ethically wrong to oppress another human being and prevent him or her from living a free, transcendent life. In an interview by Erwin B. Mee, when Dattani was asked about Nitin, a character in *Bravely Fought the Queen*, he answered saying, "Almost all gay people are married in the conventional sense, so I think there are invisible issues which need to be brought out and addressed" (Multani, 157). He, thus, has opened up to a better appropriation and recognition of the lapses and excesses of the "non-heterosexuals" (not valid now) in his first radio play, *Do the Needful*. This is just an endeavor to a deconstructive reading of Dattani's *Do the Needful*. In 1996, he wrote it for the BBC which was first broadcasted by BBC Radio on 14 August, 1997 and was directed by Sally Avens.

In *Do the Needful*, an "unconventional" and "romantic comedy", the playwright has confronted his readers to a mismatched couple. They are the central characters, viz-a-viz, the boy Alpesh, a gay and the girl Lata, in love with a Muslim terrorist and they have submitted to the pressures built up by the society in general and their parents in particular. There is also a beautiful blend of the city buzz of Mumbai with the calm landscape of rural southern countryside of Bangalore, with a "clean country air" smelling tamarind. Therefore, the setting of the play is partly Mumbai and partly Bangalore as in almost all his plays the setting is the same. Dattani, through his play, has brought in notice the true and contemporary urban and rural India. The main characters around whom the play revolves, are shown struggling for mental and physical liberty which seemed difficult in a phallocentric and heterosexual society of India. Both of them agreed to go for a marriage arranged by their parents so that they could "do the needful", which actually is an expression used in South Asian meaning, "do that which is necessary", with the respectful implication that the other party is trusted to understand what needs doing "without being given detailed instructions". A critical attention to a minute scrutiny of the texture of the play confirms a subtle employment of the technical devices like the 'thought' technique by the playwright in describing the thought process of the characters of the play. In other words the interior monologue of the main characters in the play provided us with a brilliant skill of the playwright while using this method in conveying things to the audience. But the paper predominantly meanders through levels of consciousness of the characters of the play mainly Alpesh and Lata, who willy-nilly have set to find their way in a society of conventions and taboos imposed on them by the system they were the part of. On the one hand, if the former stood taking a step ahead and going against the tide of heterosexuality, the latter very much geared up, giving liberty to the feeling of love to rule her in dismantling the myth of religious boundaries.

The play opens up with a telephonic conversation between Alpesh Patel who is "thirty plus and divorced" and is also a gay, with someone at Slim Gym. It was then when he mentioned Trilok, his gay companion as when he said, "Er, when will Trilok be free? He knows exactly where my tight spots are…" (Dattani,

119). From the interior we hear Lata Gowda's telephonic talk asking about Salim, the terrorist she was in love with. She is "twenty-four and notorious". On the one hand, when both of them were busy thinking about their companions, Patels (Gujaratis) and Marasu Vokkaliga Gowdas (Kannadigas), were busy in arranging a marriage between Alpesh and Lata (their wards). The playwright has resorted to a curious matrimonial alliance between two communities in an Indian milieu. The situation was difficult when the audience came across an inter community arranged marriage, and became more difficult when they find that both the parties were helplessly yielding to the complications with their wards. Somehow they were confused with their ability to presume that which was unacceptable. Unconsciously they were actually conscious of the difficulty which could arise if this marriage was performed. But everything was at God's risk as both the parties anticipated the satisfaction of their children. Both the families not only were culturally different but were also not seemingly alike. There are references available to their cultural difference in the play, e.g. reference to "clean country air", and Devraj Gowda mentioning "sambhar and rasam with tamarind", and at the same time guessing the taste of Patels saying, "Your dishes are mostly sweet, I think..." (Dattani, 138). In spite of the differences a mutual agreement is made between the two parties keeping with the need of the hour and in doing the needful. Talking about the cultural clash and anguish related to the industrial progress between the locals and the outsiders; where the locals implied Gowdas, and the outsiders were Patels, they say:

> Chandrakant Patel—I can understand why they must hate us.
>
> Devraj Gowda—They hate change, that is all.
>
> Chandrakant Patel—.... You have every reason to hate us.
>
> Devraj Gowda—No, no, you misunderstand....
>
> Chandrakant Patel—(Overriding his protest). But you can still consider a proposal from us for your daughter. I understand there will be reasons for not seeking a groom

> in your own community. We are also in a...similar situation. But it must be so difficult for you....
>
> Devraj Gowda—Who can stop change...I...I...don't know. I know my parents and my forefathers will be hurt very badly, and I am...betraying them, but...my daughter's happiness is most important. Please, sir, please accept my daughter. (Dattani, 2000: 47)

There is a kind of a double disillusionment. The harshness of the social conventions and the anguish of the muted, whose free wills are under constraints, represent the problems of healthy socio-cultural practices. Most obviously the audiences' minds are conquered with the thoughts of a South Indian notorious bride, and a groom who was self-righteous in being a gay. Talking to Trilok in thoughts about Lata he says:

> She was waiting for me to say something. May be I should have told her about you. After all, she was descent enough to bring up her Salman or Salim whatever. At that very moment, I imagine, our parents were sort of clinching the deal. (Dattani, 2000: 49)

But the situation was lucid as both of them agreed to a relationship with their culture and hence decided to get married beyond their differences keeping with *Teri bhi chup, meri bhi chup*. This didn't mean that they were happy in leading a life together, they were rather happy in sharing a space with each other. As Gothlin, a Swedish, in a chapter, "The Phenomenological Existentialism of Jean Paul Sartre", in the book *Sex and Existence: Simon de Beauvoir's The Second Sex*, has said of Sartre's most controversial concepts—'Bad Faith', which "describes various ways in which the human being tries to avoid the insight of freedom, and thus, to evade anguish", it is:

> What is decisive is whether, in bad faith, one flees from the insight of freedom, or whether in good faith, one attempts to live with this insight. The latter means being conscious of the fact that one must create one's life and character although one can never be it; this also means accepting that bad faith can never entirely be avoided. (Gothlin, 1996: 144)

Sartre's controversial concept of 'bad faith' when applied on the characters in the play we find that it very often is present in them and surely could not be entirely avoided. To a much extent the characters have fled from the restrictions imposed by the 'bad faith'. Thus, following what 'good faith' implies we find that marrying a gay will help Lata to carry on with Salim surreptitiously, and will also cater Alpesh in continuing his relationship with Trilok. Ultimately at the end of the play the characters chose to be themselves. They kept up the façade of a happy married life, but at another end they fully deviated from the conceptualization of 'bad faith'. As for good faith, keeping in view Sartre, the Swedish writer has also said:

> The ideal of good faith is being what we are, not escaping from it. But because human consciousness 'is what it is not, and not what it is', this is never possible. (Gothlin, 1996: 144)

Alpesh's "homophobic dream", in other words, his homophobic consciousness thus, made impossible possible. Going with the 'good faith' his dreams turned real when in marrying Lata he found no obstacle in continuing with Trilok (the gay companion), and thus not escaping from what he is. He, in the process therefore, didn't conceal the truth, which the person in a 'bad faith' does. The play thus is attractive and invites audience to watch an unusual setting in an Indian milieu where homosexuality is a stigma and the society can only be propitious by the elimination of gays. But simultaneously the play has also startled the audience and has left them awe struck, for the playwright has privileged the individual's free will and given voice to the unheard voices. The playwright didn't miss to speak the audiences' minds also, and this he has done through the character of a coconut vendor Marriappa who addressing Patels, the outsiders, says:

> Coconut Vendor—Namaskara, sar! How do you like our village?
>
> Alpesh—What is he saying?
>
> Coconut Vendor—Don't you speak Kannad? Where are they from? He looks a little old for our Latamma.

> Prema Gowda—Dev pay him off so the man can leave.
>
> Coconut Vendor—You are all modern big people.... You should find a nice Gowda boy for our Latamma.
>
> Devraj Gowda—This is not your Grandfather's time, you fool.
>
> Coconut Vendor—Yes, yes. You are all doctors. Modern big people. Giving so much freedom to your children. (Dattani, 2000: 140)

Hence, also in the case of this coconut vendor Mariappa, we find a playful role of 'bad and good faith'. Mariappa in the play emphasizes the serious disadvantages of adopting the modern culture. He actually hated it, one for a reason that his daughter ran away to Bombay and surely would have ended up in a brothel, and the second for his land is facing the aftermaths of civilization. Mariappa thus showed his anguish towards these "big modern people" by beating the drum. At one point Lata tells Alpesh, "Mariappa beats the drum when he is really angry with the whole world" (Dattani, 2000: 42). Other than speaking the audiences' minds, the playwright has also shifted our attention to the very tension which prevailed between the industrial advancements and the rural countryside. In a conversation with Alpesh about the Sugarcane-eating contests, Devraj Gowda recalls:

> My poor uncle's family, paid a pittance by the BDA. We had to bribe all kinds of officers to keep our land. All this acquiring in the name of progress. Filthy greedy scoundrels in the government, I tell you. (Dattani, 2000: 138)

He further elaborates:

> Devraj Gowda—It is all because of those bloody illegal industrialists! They don't even spare our Halli! Siphoning the electricity from the poles! All crooks, I tell you! All of them do all this in their own state. Let them do all this in their own state.
>
> Alpesh (quietly)—Not all industrialists are thieves. Sir.

> Devraj Gowda—I know. It is all those corrupt government officers who are encouraging all this just to line their pockets. Rotten to the core! Our country has gone to the dogs because of them. (Dattani, 145)

The environmental hazards accompanied by the development of industries in these parts of country also invited the wrath of the countrymen for the "excessive consumption of water and electricity". This is again well evident in Marriappa's speech. He says:

> Coconut Vendor—Those sons of demons! Who asked them to come here? (Shouts after the car). Go away! We don't want your money! Go! (Spitting loudly in anger). I am a son of this soil, this is my land! We don't want you, you son's of whores! Born in the most inauspicious time! (To Devraj Gowda). And to them. Aiyo! Big people! Modern people! (Fades out as he walks away with his cycle). Kaliyuga! Kaliyuga! Our mother is being raped and her sons are watching...! (Dattani, 2003: 141)

Not only Dattani has made aloud the major debates of our society but also has interwoven the fabric of his play in such a way that every current challenge receives a well pronunciation. It is in this spirit that the playwright has offered a speech to the subalterns in the play, viz-a-viz. Alpesh, Lata, and Marriappa. He also has tried to dawn the awareness, fight the social conventions invariably, and has been successful in achieving the same, for the characters demanding liberty in the end have kept up being what they are in accepting the imposed socio-cultural paradigms, and then twisting them in their own way. The metaphysics of this utopian society foregrounds the opposition between the ideal and the grotesque. And thus it represses that which is a variation from the norm. Subalterns in the play, mainly Alpesh and Lata, have revolted against the norms by doing the needful in the end. This desire for liberation has enhanced in them the tendency to flight instead of justifying their existence to the society. Transcendence is thus, achieved by being the 'Beings', attempting to contradict what the society offers. They have at one point accepted the norms and at other point condemned it. This has been the most authentic and human in their ability in doing the needful by characterizing things differently for themselves, thus, giving a blow to the heterosexual society which is utopian, where people like Alpesh have to accept the position of the 'Other'. The play is thus, a tribute to the dramatic vision of the playwright who has given a stage to the lives of the unheard.

Works Cited

Agarwal, Beena. *Mahesh Dattani's Plays: A New Horizon in Indian English Theatre*. Jaipur: Book Enclave, 2008. Print.

Aver Back, Nina. *Romantic Imprisonment: Women and Other Outcast*. New York: Columbia UP, 1985. Print.

Bhasim, Kamla. *Understanding Gender*. New Delhi: Pauls Press, 2000. Print.

Butler, Judith. *Gender Trouble: Feminism and the Subversion of Identity*. New York: Routledge, 1990. Print.

Chaudhuri, Asha Kuthari. *Mahesh Dattani: An Introduction*. New Delhi: Foundation Books, 2005. Print.

Dattani, Mahesh. *Collected Plays: Critical Perspectives*. New Delhi: Penguin Books, 2000. Print.

Glover, David and Cora Kaplan. *Genders: The New Critical Idiom*. London and New York: Routledge, 2007. Print.

Gothlin, Eva Lundgren. *Sex and Existence: Simon de Beauvoir's The Second Sex*. Trans. Linda Schenck. Hanover and London: University Press of New England, 1996. Print.

Multani, Angelie. (ed.). *Mahesh Dattani's Plays: Critical Perspectives*. New Delhi: Pencraft International, 2007. Print.

Poovey, Mary. *Uneven Development: The Ideological Work of Gender in Mid-Victorian England*. Chicago: The University Press of Chicago, 1988. Print.

11

Lifting the Veil, the Woman Speaks: A Critical Appraisal of Dattani's *Thirty Days in September* and *Highway*

Mustabshira Siddiqui

> Main 9 saal ki thi…wo imported chocolates late the… mere uncle…mujhe god me bitha kar pyaar karte the… aur akele me bathroom ke andar phir god me bithate the aur pyar karte the, cheekhti thi main aur mera munh band kar dete the, "ssshh, ssshh bas bas ho gya, meri gudiya best ladki hai tu duniya ki meri gudiya…" baar baar aate the, cheekhti thi main…"kisi se kehna nai"… ek din maine mummy ko bol diya…mummy ne kaha, "ssh ssh kisi se kehna nai, theek hai"…uske baad maine kisi se nai kaha…. (*Highway*, 2014 Movie)

(I was nine years old…he used to bring me imported chocolates…made me sit in his lap and loved me…and then in alone he took me to bathroom and again made me sit in his lap and again made love to me…I used to shout, he used to shut my mouth, "Ssh ssh…it's done, it's done my baby doll; you are the best girl of this world…" He came again and again…I shouted and shouted … Don't tell anyone…One day I told this to my mother, "Ssh, ssh don't tell this to anyone", my mother replied…then I did not tell anyone.)

Mahesh Dattani, an Indian English Sahitya Akademi Award winning playwright, has concentrated his critical stare at depicting the issues under the carpet of the Indian society that are often brushed aside in spite of the fact that these are like plague eating out all social and the moral values. In his play, *Thirty Days in September*. Mahesh Dattani has dramatized the most heinous crime, child sexual abuse. Dealing with the child incest, the play throws light on the consequences of the forced sexual relation on the individual's psyche, which takes a hazardous turn with the passage of time, than the issue itself, especially on a child's psyche. The protagonist of the play, Mala, is molested by her maternal uncle (mother's brother) before reaching her puberty. Her mother does not raise voice against her daughter's molestation. As Mala grows older, she becomes mentally and physically vulnerable and sexually addicted. The play also throws light on mother's silence against her daughter's molestation resulting in a conflict between the relationship of mother and daughter which ends with the mother's confession that she herself was sexually abused and molested by the same person in her childhood.

Mahesh Dattani, born in Gujarat, becomes the first English language playwright to win several awards and teaches theatre courses at the summer sessions programme of Portland State University, Oregon, USA, and conducts workshops regularly at his studio and elsewhere. He also writes plays for BBC Radio. *Thirty Days in September* has touched hearts and conscience of everyman. It is a play full of sensitivity and powerful feelings touching every heart without offending anyone's sensibilities; it tries to bring home the horror and the pain within the framework of a very identifiable mother-daughter relationship. It also lays bare the trauma of a girl child when she is given counseling sessions.

The present paper explores the transformation in her psyche as an independent, liberated and self assured Mala after the counseling session in the beginning of the play that can be noticed through her following remark:

> Mala: Mala Khatri. February 2004 ... (Listening to the counselor) Why not? ... I do not hesitate to use my real name now. Let people know. There's nothing to hide. Not for me. After all, it is he who must hide. He should

> change his name, not me. It is he who must avoid being recognized. In people's homes, at parties, hopefully even on streets. He should look the other way when someone spots him anywhere on this planet. And I can make that happen. I have the power to do that now. If I use my real name...(sighing, thinking about it almost as if it is a pleasant memory). I wish he was here now, so I could see his face when I tell him I have nothing to hide. Because I know it was not my fault.... Now. I know now. (Act I, 88)

A play about love, incest and betrayal, *Thirty Days in September,* treats the sensitive and assumed to be a taboo issue of child sexual abuse. It endeavors to lift the 'veil of silence' which surrounds child sexual abuse and incestuous relations in Indian society. It builds on the trauma of Mala who lives with the haunting memories of her abused past. Her abuser—her uncle "subconsciously lives with her all the time, as part of her dirty reflections". According to Beena Agrawal:

> Mala, the protagonist, is the victim of this abuse but she maintains silence against injustice. As soon as she comes to the stage of adolescence, she finds that the world is hostile and human relationship is a betrayal. (*Mahesh Dattani's Plays: A New Horizon in Indian Theatre*. 2008: 118)

Her abuser Vinay, damages her natural growth, deters her from pursuing her love interests beyond the ominous 30-days period and scars her soul every now and then, making her feel hollow, emotionless and mechanical in sex. As Mala shatters under the psychological pain imposed on her by the abuser, her mother watches silently, carrying her own pain—suffering mutely. In this regard Asha Kuthari Chaudhuri observes: "Child sexual abuse spans a range of problems, but it is this complicity of the family through silence and a lack of protest that is the ultimate betrayal for the abused" (*Contemporary Indian Writers in English: Mahesh Dattani—An Introduction*, 2005: 73).

The major and most heinous issue that Dattani has raised is an attack on contemporary postmodern upper-class cultured society. The issue strikes the mind of not only the playwrights of social concern but also of film and movie makers having a concern for society. Imtiaz Ali is such a movie maker in India. His recent movie *Highway* is also about child sexual abuse. Like that of Dattani's Mala in *Thirty Days in September,* the movie deals with story of a girl, Veera's (Alia Bhatt's) sexual abuse. When she was out for a stroll at highway with her fiancé on the way Veera is abducted by bandits in mask. Any way succeeds in making an escape. But she has a very interesting journey as she feels that being held hostage by a band of quasi-radical bandits is actually less constructing than upper-class bourgeois life. Her ease with bandits throws them all for a bit of loop, and gradually chips away at Mahabir's (Randeep Hooda) monolithic, humourless exterior and before he knows it, he is taken with her incongruous pleasantness, and he begins to see her as a young woman rather than an upper class. He is also taken aback when Veera reveals her story of sexual abuse by her own uncle. He is surprised to find out the darker side of upper-class women. Here comes the turning point in his (Mahabir's) life. The movie ends with complete denoument as Veera unveils her perpetrator in front of her family and goes away to live a separate life.

The plot of the movie *Highway* and the play *Thirty Days in September* is in a way similar to each other. As Veera reveals that her mother asked her not to tell anyone, one can trace Mala too have suffered the same agony on her mother's part. *Highway* reveals the dark side of upper-class women while the *Thirty Days in September* the middle-class. But it is not a story of upper and middle-class girls; it is actually the complete society which is a part of this game. Mala and Veera are not merely characters from a play and movie they are the types from the society one lives in. One breathes in the same kind of atmosphere and is sexual abuse never feels the urge to make it lively and cure the crime of sexual abuse. These issues always lay under the carpet and no one dares to voice against them. The hypocrite society never raises a voice against all these odds and keeps on turning its deaf ears towards these issues. Mahesh Dattani and Imtiaz Ali are the real people who question on this hypocrite society and try to bring this problem on the stage and urge people to stand against such crimes.

Before proceeding further let us know what constitutes child sexual abuse. It involves conditioning a child for sexual activity by forcing, tricking, threatening, emotionally blackmailing, or pressurizing. It can be not only physical but verbal, emotional or sexual and occurs when an adult or an older or even more knowledgeful child uses a child for his sexual pleasure. The abuse often begins gradually and increases over time. It includes sexual touching and fondling or exposing children to adult sexual activity including pornographic movies and photographs, etc. Kendall and Tackett have also described the sexual abuse in following way:

> Sexual relations of any kind perpetrated by biologically or non-biologically related person functioning in the role of a family member. Other trusted adults could also sexually abuse children and teenagers. These include parents, uncles, aunts, siblings, stepparents, grandparents, coaches, baby sitters, clergy and teachers. (http://www.livestrong.com/article/12505-sexual-abuseincest/) (Kendall-Tackett, 1993)

Dattani is a close observer of society. Themes of his plays emerge from social conditions and not from his speculation. The adversities of society, savage behaviour of educated and cultured gentry and psychological acceptability of evils always strike his mind and reaction we get a variety of his plays. What affects him is expressed in a conversation with Anitha Santhanam, Dattani:

> It's the silence and the betrayal of the family that affects me the most. Like in this case, the mother knew that her daughter was being sexually abused by her uncle, but still chooses to keep quiet. It's the silence that makes the abused feel betrayed. ("It's the silence that affects me most", 2001)

Exploring the heart distorting problem, Mahesh Dattani raises valid concerns and constructs a world of optimism and morals where the wrong can stand corrected and resurrection of barbaric faith is possible. And this happens when Deepak raises his concern for his love's sake to Mala to unveil the past and attend the counseling sessions, it is, there, at counseling session that Mala could tell someone from outside what she buried in her psyche long ago and yearned to talk about it to someone. Deepak, Mala's boyfriend, becomes the rescuer of their lives. He dares to unmask the evil, even at the cost of his love for Mala.

In *Highway* too same thing happens with Veera. She feels unburdened after she unveils the mask of the hypocrite society and reveals the truth to a real man Mahabir. She too, like Dattani's Mala, was tortured by the same hypocrisy by her mother's part who always warned her not to tell about it to anyone. The sealed lips only could open their voice when she got a real man—a man with human heart from a working class. As Mala opens her mouth in front of her boyfriend to discuss her plight at last she feels secured and confident similarly Veera too attains her courage and confidence with Mahabir's support. This is not a story of Mala and Veera only, they are representative of savagely educated contemporary society, there are many Malas and Veeras who fall victims of this horrible reality which no one wants to talk about, even not the women themselves.

In the play *Thirty Days in September*, Dattani portrays Mala as a victim of incest with hazardous consequences on her. On top of that she is also the daughter of a victim of incest and abuse. Throughout the play both Mala and her mother are collapsed disturbed and angry in their conversation. The daughter shows more behavioural problems arising out of incest and sexual abuse. She could not live normally and behaved in a very strange way because of having physical relationship with any man who comes her way. Even her boyfriend could not understand her behaviour when she rejects him after his proposal in spite of his great relationship with her. It happens because of the violation of a trusted relationship with the perpetrator who is none else but her own maternal uncle, Vinay. Mala is sexually tortured by Vinay several times during every summer vacation. She has great expectations from her mother, Shanta, for emotional support and understanding. But whenever the daughter came out with her woes in front of her mother, she pretended it to be something insignificant and never responded positively to strengthen her emotionally and never raised a voice against Mala's abuser.

On the contrary, she immediately fed her with her favourite dish of *alu parathas* and stuffed her till she was full. This gave

Mala a temporary relief as she started feeling that that was the cure for her restless heart. This created a gulf between the two of them and it keeps on increasing day by day until Deepak goes to Mala's house to her mother and asks her to tell about Mala's problem which the mother refuses to tell but feels an attachment towards Deepak who confesses his true love for Mala and asks for her help to reach to Mala's strange behaviour towards him. Though Shanta was completely aware of the terrible reality that Mala was suffering from but always avoided her questions and whenever Mala insisted she rushed to seek help from Lord Krishna. Mala hates her mother's attitude for rushing to take support from Lord Krishna. Shanta wants to help Mala by praying continuously which results in contrary and makes Mala mad as she throws out the idol of Krishna out of the house and she condemns her mother for shattering her soul:

> Where were you when he locked the door to your bed room while I was napping in there? Where were you during those fifteen minutes when he was destroying my soul? Fifteen minutes every day of my summer holidays, add them up. Fifteen minutes multiplied by thirty or thirty-one or whatever. That's how long or how little it took for you to send me to hell for the rest of my life! (*Collected Plays* II. 2005, Act III, 133)

When her mother confesses the crime and tells her own traumatic past Mala freezes. She feels paralyzed when her mother tells her about the financial help they were getting since Mala's father left them. Mala is stunned after hearing this horrible reality from her mother, "Mala, I am sorry; I should have told you but...the money that we kept receiving after your father left us, was from your uncle" (*Collected Plays* II. 2005, Act II, 115). Mala's uncle bought her mother's silence, that's why Shanta dared not to raise voice against the molestation of Mala by her own brother. Again at the meeting he tries to buy the silence of Mala's mother by writing the property in her name, when Deepak tries to persuade them to speak the truth; "he bought your silence. So that you can never tell anyone what he did to your daughter!" (*Collected Plays* II. 2005, Act III, 133). Unlike her mother's plight, Mala, in support of Deepak, appears more confident at the last counseling session:

> Mala: (Self assured and easy). I feel I want to tell it to people who would understand. It's like starting all over again. It's like you never had those scars.
>
> Mala's voice on tape: ...my father left us, for another woman....
>
> Mala: It's like taking off the bandages on your face after a bloody car crash that left your face all scarred beyond recognition, as if you didn't have a face at all. To wake up after many years, as if from a coma...and let the bandages come off...and suddenly discover a whole new face again. All of a sudden you feel that you are—entitled to life. (*Collected Plays* II. 2005, Act II, 113)

Hence, the play ends with a terrific note instead of a question. Are they ready to unveil the veil? If yes, they have to do it themselves. No one will come for their rescue in this society; she has to fight her battle alone. And prove herself that she is not a commodity to be used, abused and thrown out. The moment a woman tries to assert her existence, society abuses her but when comes out with identity same society respects her. It's a bit hard journey but full of existence and independence. Though Mala gts that identity but she could not shed her traumatic past unless she speaks openly about it in front of her perpetrator and lover. The same thing happens with Veera in Highway as she reveals her heart in front of Mahabir who eventually becomes her lover and feels a great relief after confessing it to him.

Both Veera and Mala not only reveal the truth boldly rather comments on their uncles publically at home and outside. She asks him for his imported chocolates rather she taunts him in front of her family whether he carried his foreign chocolates for her today or not? And when he answers in positive she again taunts him that where he is planning to give it to her? Whether in bathroom or in bedroom? The man goes away leaving the family stunned and muted. She leaves her house to live on her own as she has nothing to do in the high strata of her parents who could not protect her in her own home.

For Mahesh Dattani's *Thirty Days in September*, 'The Hindu' published a review by Romesh Chander that says:

He hits the women hard until they hit the rock bottom. Finally, there is no way but to come up—face the wrongs and dare to correct them, notwithstanding the challenges the process of correction entails. By marking a daring departure from norm, the play ensures that we, as a society, no longer take comfort in the routine of uttering word "incest" in gutless undertones. The play also brings us closer to the reality of abused children—pleasure does apart from their pain, but finally the consequence of dangerous games can only be dangerous. Our only way to fight danger is to recognize it and crush with generous doses of brutality lest we are ready to condemn innocence to lifelong death. (Romesh Chander, Editor, *The Hindu*, March 30, 2007).

Works Cited

Agrawal, Beena. *Mahesh Dattani's Plays: A New Horizon in Indian Theatre*. Jaipur: Book Enclave, 2008. Print.

Ali, Imtiyaz. *Highway* (Movie). February, 2014.

Bergen, R.K. "Sexual Victimization of Children: Incest and Child Sexual Abuse", *Issues in Time Violence*. ed. Newbury Park, CA: Sage.

Chaudhuri, Asha Kuthari. *Contemporary Indian Writers in English: Mahesh Dattani: An Introduction*. New Delhi: Foundation, 2005. Print.

Chander, Romesh. Editor, *The Hindu*, March 30, 2007. Print.

Dattani, Mahesh. *Collected Plays II*. New Delhi: Penguin, 2005. Print.

——. Interview by Anitha Santhanam. "It's the Silence that Affects Me Most" 2001. Web. http://www.maheshdattani.com *The Hindu*, Mar 30, 2007)

Multani, Angelie. (ed.). "Introduction". *Mahesh Dattani's Plays: Critical Perspectives*. New Delhi: Pencraft International, 2007. Print.

http://www.hinduonnet.com/thehindu/fr/2007/03/30/stories/2007033001470300.htm

http://www.livestrong.com/article/12505-sexual -abuse-incest/.20/06/2014.

http://en.wikipedia.org/wiki/child_sexual_abuse.21/06/2014.

12

Relocating the Margins: A Study of Alternate Sexuality in Dattani's Plays

Preeti Singh

Mahesh Dattani's plays come as a challenge to our conservative Indian society. Other than feminism and gender-discrimination he brings to the fore the issue of alternate sexuality. It strikes at the root of concept of continuity of civilization through the promotion of idea of centrality of heterosexual relationship in society, where the homosexuals are subjected to exclusion and contempt. In his plays Dattani provides space to the 'queer' people and queer sexuality as he subscribes to the view that sexuality is a matter of choice from one's own position and it is defined by an individual in his specific case. Queer means "...to be a transgressor, to go against the grain and trespass onto forbidden ground, aiming thereby to expose the fraudulent artifice of mainstream society's most centrally constitutive taboos and prohibitions" (Schoene, 285). The coining of the phrase "Queer theory" is attributed to Teresa de Lauretis, during a conference on gay and lesbian sexualities, held in 1990 at the University of California; in Santa Cruz. Queer theory explores the categorization of gender and sexuality. The theory interrogates the solidified segregation into normative and deviant sexuality. This paper discusses Dattani's plays that deal with the homosexual, the ostracized and marginalized segment of society, within the middle class, where heterosexuality epitomizes the normal and deviation from it is considered as an aberration in the gendered category of the social set up.

Deviance from the specific behavioural standard or ways in which people are supposed to act, is regarded as the violation of those norms. It is considered as a failure to conform to social or cultural norms. Heterosexuality, which refers to romantic or sexual attraction between the members of opposite sex is a norm and deviance from it is deemed to be an act of trespassing or ethical perversion. Thus, the alternate sexual orientation of an individual that is homosexuality or bisexuality is considered as the deviance from the norm and unnatural. Although homosexual behaviour is regarded as abnormal, cross-cultural and historical studies, qualify that it has existed throughout human history and probably in all human cultures on a global scale. During antiquity and in numerous cultures, evidence exists of same-sex relations between men and women. Social attitudes towards same-sex relationships have varied over time and place. Many societies did not forbid consensual same-sex rather surprisingly celebrated it, some took it to be casual, and some considered the practice as a minor sin while at certain places it was proscribed under penalty of death. Since time immemorial and within all cultures of the world, gays, lesbians, transgendered and inter-sexed people have been described, acknowledged and even accommodated within society. By all accounts, whether their members were positively accommodated or negatively suppressed within each of their respective societies, the alternative gender subcultures have always naturally existed in one form or another.

Dattani undauntingly deals with the issue of homosexuality, a peripheral one that remained latent because people do not accept the concept to be Indian nor that it exists in India. He preoccupies himself of speaking affirmatively about a subject that is considered literally unspeakable. One of the main ways in which homosexuals are marginalized is by ignoring them. They are rendered invisible by society. People rule it out as Indian for they consider it a Western phenomenon and the 'West' is blamed for introducing deviant sexual practices. Homosexual behaviour has been illegal in most countries for several centuries. It was only in recent decades that a number of nations began to implement legislative reforms which allow for certain consensual homosexual acts. Thus, it demands loads of grit on the part of a playwright to deal with such an issue as it was a closeted phenomenon in terms of representation; it was not expressed overtly. As Dattani himself says in an interview that "You can talk about feminism, because in a way that is accepted. But you can't talk about gay issues that's not Indian, it doesn't happen here" (Mee, 163).

Nevertheless, various historical literary evidences indicate that homosexuality has been prevalent across the Indian subcontinent throughout history. His plays focus on both the marginal issues and the people. Dattani locates the peripheral issue of alternate sexuality, which has been marginalized like certain marginalized sections of the society, and presents the issue through his theatrical art. In Indian context monogamous procreative sex in marriage is considered to be the only kind of practice prevalent and permissible. Sexuality in India in any form is hardly discussed overtly. While various evidences belie the claim as Ruth Vanita in her book *Gandhi's Tiger and Sita's Smile* claims that "Like the erotic temple sculptures at Khajuraho and Konark, the fourth century *Kamasutra* constitute irrefutable evidence that the whole range of sexual behaviour was known and practiced in India" (269). There are other Hindu texts that mention homosexuality, asserting the fact that homosexuality did exist in India. In *Same-Sex Love in India: Readings from Literature and History*, Ruth Vanita asserts that:

> Our study suggests that at most times and places in pre-nineteenth-century India, love between women and between men, even when disapproved of, was not actively persecuted. As far as we know, no one has ever been executed for homosexuality in India. (xviii)

Nevertheless, homosexuality remained unmentionable until the controversy around the film 'Fire', about lesbianism, by Deepa Mehta; a Canada based Indian director, in 1998 created a furore. This issue was never spoken of by any of the organizations, or the sections of society ever before. The film was damned by right-wing Hindu nationalists as evidence of the corruption of Indian culture by the West. Shiv Sena and other political and religious groups criticized the film for its unusual theme. They declared homosexuality 'western' and merely an 'upper-class' phenomenon in India. Cinema halls were vandalized and posters defaced in many parts of India and death threats were made against the director and the actresses, and this became a national agitation, although the film won accolades in the West. The irony of the fact is that "However, here 'at home' in India, the director explicitly denied that the film had a lesbian theme, quickly clarified to the press that she was heterosexual, and reportedly said that she would be devastated if her daughter turned out to be lesbian" (Campaign For Lesbian Rights, 561). Public discussion of homosexuality in India has been inhibited by the fact that sexuality in any form is rarely discussed openly. The entrance of the lesbian into Indian culture also intervenes in a changing public culture in which sex is marked differently from the previous decades. There has been a substantial shift in attitudes to sexuality with the economic liberalization of the 1990s and the rise in consumer class in the 1980s and 1990s. HIV/AIDS has been one of the most significant factors in breaching Indian society's powerful taboo on public discussion about sexuality, in the process creating an unprecedented opportunity for multiple sexuality discourses. This new dialogue challenges narrow constructions of patriarchal gender relations and heteronormativity. This opportunity is the new visibility of formerly marginalized sexual and transgender communities. As in an interview Ashok Row Kavi, asserts that:

> In ancient India, transgendered people were recognized by nuns and Buddhists in the monastery as a sacred sexual minority. Throughout the Vedas and in Middle Eastern literature, many texts talk about feminine males. India drifted from its acceptance of homosexuality because of the influence of colonial British education. Accepting homosexuality isn't something new for India—but we have to recover that tradition. (2008)

Mahesh Dattani is ahead of his times as he created a gay character in his play *Bravely Fought the Queen* (1991). This was for the first time that a gay individual registered its presence on the stage openly in a drama. It was a courageous task on the part of Dattani because as Sohini Ghosh in her foreword to Ruth Vanita's *Gandhi's Tiger and Sita's Smile* avers that, "Today, the silence around queer sexuality is decisively broken. Yet the public discourse around sexuality in India continues to be deeply fraught" (Scene, iii). Nitin, a closeted homosexual, in *Bravely Fought the Queen*, is conned by his lover Praful. He tricks Nitin into marrying his sister, Alka, who is ignorant of her husband's sexual proclivities. Nitin's latent homosexuality leads him to be ineffectual, while his elder brother dominates and controls the family and business matters, for he is the decision-maker and the authoritarian figure. Praful being a manipulator controls and affects Nitin's life, in spite of being absent from the scene. Queer theory challenges hegemonizing heterosexual norm, and professes to articulate the alternate preferences. Homosexuality which was previously a silent space, queer theory has opened up space for its articulation by opposing against stratified sexual identities. Dattani here brings in the problems faced by an individual as one dares not to come out to family members for the fear of denial, disgust and all the negative feelings they may have in regard to the issue. Ruth Vanita expresses it efficiently on Ashok Row Kavi's 'coming out', in her own words:

> I respect Ashok greatly. In fact, when he came out in a popular Indian magazine many years ago, I thought 'great!' I grew up with many of the classic gay feelings of loneliness, feeling different from others, cut-offness and so on. Ashok's openness has encouraged many gay Indians to come to terms with their sexuality. (Ayyar, 2002)

In *Do the Needful* (1997) Dattani dwells on the same subject from another perspective. Once again the institution of marriage is used as a mere façade to hide the complexities of modern life in India. This play deals with the problem of love and homosexuality, simultaneously. Lata, the female protagonist, who belongs to a Kannadiga family, is in love with a Muslim, who happens to be a Kashmiri terrorist; on the other hand is Alpesh, a Gujarati boy, who is homosexual and divorced form the locus of the play. The play traces how both of them manage to have their own ways. Dattani underscores the fact that two heterogeneous groups in respect to communities reluctantly come together, in spite of major differences pertaining to wealth, power, food habits and other minor nuances, in order to avert the cultural cataclysm and collapse, in their own context. For them it is preferable to get into inter-community marriage, to a certain extent rather than facing the rejection of society by allowing their children to be transgressors as per social standards. "The common oppressor in the picture is the patriarchal structures that refuse to allow any space for the growth of individual identities beyond its periphery" (Chaudhuri, 96). Dattani highlights that the individuals are forced to conform to the stratified norm for lack of choice; they could not find any other way out to deal with the situation. Dattani points out the issue that such characters may be existing in our midst and society is at ease to assume that it is not an Indian concept. The playwright scrutinizes the situation impartially and tries to make the point that the stringency in social norms and stratified heteronormative sexual arrangement leads to and provokes the ostentatious life pattern, resulting in the severe violations and sins of committing sacrilege. As in play the two distraught characters under the pretext of a pious institution like marriage, find their own ways to serve the personal ends. Ironically, society promotes such acts.

On a Muggy Night in Mumbai (1998) is another startling tragi-comedy dealing with the travails and trifles of the gay community. Dattani presents the grey veracities, the evils that occur in the modern urban families in the metropolitan cities. In spite of the unconventional theme the play is moored in family set-up, making it a point that family is an inseparable part of Indian culture. The play ingeniously deals with the various shades of gay life. Dattani points out the ghettoization of these individuals because of rejection and marginalization in a country like India where such relationships are considered as unnatural, loathsome and impious. The gay lot nevertheless aware of all these facts happens to be so what they are. They all are complex characters who cannot be understood by their superficial gender preferences only. They have their own fears and fantasies, cares and apprehensions, conscience and consciousness, emotions and passions as part of their personality traits like anybody else. They have different expressions regarding their identity. A dramatic tension is orchestrated and the subterranean consciousness of each character is laid bare. The play puts forth that they are individuals in their own right in spite of the same natural inclinations, as their perceptions about the society, traditions and about their own selves are not identical to each other. Kamlesh's flat is a place where this gay group can meet openly and this group provides a deep insight into the discrepancies within this community. Kamlesh is the weak and submissive one, being jilted by his lover Prakash, who wants to be straight, feels desperate and distraught. Kamlesh gets nostalgic regarding his affair and finds himself caught up into frustration and antagonism resulting from separation from Prakash. He feels it difficult to cope with Prakash's decision and it leads to his suffering and pain. He comes in contact with Sharad; both Kamlesh and Sharad live together for some time but, unable to forget Ed or Prakash, Kamlesh dumps Sharad. Kamlesh starts seeing a psychiatrist hoping to be cured of the mental dilemma but in vain and fails to set himself straight. Ed expresses the fear and disgust for his own alternative choice and assumes a new façade of being straight as 'Ed', who fakes himself deeply in love with Kiran, Kamlesh's sister. As he cannot adjust himself to the incongruity between the external and internal and this clash leads them towards suicidal attempts. As puts Beena Agarwal:

> In both these plays, *On a Muggy Night in Mumbai* and *Do the Needful*, the dramatist while expressing his sympathy for gays who are not morally degraded but mentally sick, expose their struggle with their own inner selves. The possibility of the shared spaces common to women and homosexual is put to active use here with the identities of its protagonists. (Agrawal, 53)

Dattani delineates the complications in the life that lead to internal conflict and identity crisis. It relentlessly and sensitively interrogates and underscores the need to use dialogue as a remedy for the socially pressing issue. Family is an important unit of the Indian social fabric. Indian social system revolves around the family not merely as a single component but as a joint system where several small units cohabit within a single house and regulate and influence one another and are in turn controlled by a patriarch let us say the grandfather. Individuals are expected to marry and have children. In this context, there is little space for homosexual relationships. Only a minority of homosexuals in India express their sexuality openly while most are compelled by their family to marry and raise children. A homosexual in the family is a source of "great shame" and embarrassment. Some homosexuals come out to their family and others are ousted. While some families accept, others disown, discriminate against, ostracize and react violently to the news.

The prince of the state of Rajpipla in Gujarat, Manvendra Singh Gohil, who runs an NGO, Lakshya for gay people, is one of the most prominent gay personalities in India. He is the only person of royal lineage who publicly proclaimed his gay identity. He disclosed, in an interview, that he was initially disowned by his father and mother, although lives in the same palace, though in a separate wing; as his mother is still to accept the fact. It illustrates the fact that not only decriminalization of the homosexuality by the government is required to change the situation rather acceptance of the reality on the social and cultural level is the vital issue in a country like India.

Dattani provides centre stage to the eunuch in his play *Seven Steps Around the Fire* (1999), who meets the brutal end of one's life, because of one's gender, as it belongs to the community that is hardly, considered of importance, who exist only on the periphery. The hijra community in India, which has history of more than 4,000 years, was considered to have special powers because of its third-gender status having its own well-established 'eunuch culture'. The play underscores the irony of the fact, that the eunuchs whose presence in the birth and marriage ceremonies is considered auspicious, to grace the newly married couple, to assure parenthood, are not allowed to partake such ceremonies. They are not privileged enough to have such occurrences in their own lives.

Dattani explores the issue in the play, by means of Uma, a research scholar, daughter of V.C. of Bangalore University, wife of a police officer and daughter-in-law of Deputy Commissioner of police, presenting her as a sleuth. Dattani draws parallels between Uma and the transgendered section, for in spite of her high status; she suffers isolation because of being childless that relegates her to insignificant status, where she is expected to appease her husband and to prove herself fit for motherhood. Uma manages to empathize with eunuchs because of their marginal existence and is adamant to investigate the murder of a beautiful eunuch Kamla, a case that has been hushed up. Dattani censures the legal machinery for its insensitivity and questions the dignity of social norms. The play explores the fact that transgendered are considered as objects for throughout the play they are addressed with the pronouns, it, this thing, etc. Sexual abuse and violence, apart from being the most systematic tool for dehumanizing an individual, can be understood as a punishment for not conforming to the gender roles laid down by society. Dattani probes into their lives as most of the eunuchs in India live by begging. When Uma asks Anarkali to tell something about herself she answers sarcastically "What is there to tell? I sing with other hijras at weddings and when a child is born. People give us money otherwise I will put a curse on them (*Laughing*). As if God is on our side" (I.241).

Uma unfolds the mystery of murder of Kamla, a beautiful eunuch, in the pursuit of her research work on 'hijra' community Kamla, is burnt to death on the orders of Mr. Sharma, an influential minister, because of Kamla's secret marriage to Subbu, his son, who is deeply in love with Kamla. The matter is hushed up because of the influential position of the minister, as he is not ready to accept this relationship and considers it unnatural and unacceptable at the societal level. Dattani divulges the truth that the unacceptability on the part of mainstream society demonstrates itself in extreme form as brutal violence. "The play presents the transgendered as the victims of society which has its own fixed notions about his/her social status" (George, 146).

Dattani underlines the unjust treatment meted out to the transgendered section of society. They are denied the rudimentary right to safeguard their lives and dignity. They are the social victims who do not have a say on the social or legal level. The play foregrounds the issue that they are subjected to violence in public spaces, police stations and prisons. The harassment and surveillance by the police sometimes extends into the privacy of their homes. The discrimination based on gender and class makes them susceptible to harassment by the police. Anarkali, the accused hijra, in the play is put in a male prison and is beaten by the other prisoners. The place with the most scope for abuse is the police station where the police, on a regular basis, encroach upon all canons of civilized behaviour by physically, sexually and verbally abusing and demeaning hijras. Uma extends her empathy and sets out to prove the innocence of Anarkali, the accused, with the help of Munswamy, the constable. She succeeds in bringing out the truth, by suffusing a sense of conviction and acceptance in Anarkali and Champa other transsexuals, who agree to help her in the process.

The playwright discloses various myths and beliefs regarding the hijra community. Although they take their own time to establish rapport, Uma eventually succeeds in convincing them and offers sisterhood. Their skeptical attitude towards the mainstream society is emphasized when Champa asks Uma "you see us also as society, no?" (I.23). Their paranoiac attitude towards the society is born out of the social and legal apathy that leaves them alone, no one to look up to or to give voice to their gloom and suppression, bound to the limitations constructed by the Indian social set-up. Subbu and Kamla; are both forced to meet horrifying ends, because of their divergent sexual preferences. Kamla is punished for transgression by registering the prominence in Subbu's life, while Subbu moves towards suicide as a result of his homosexual proclivity.

The main factor behind the violence is that society is not able to come to terms with the fact that hijras do not conform to the accepted gender divisions. Despite the supposedly sanctioned place in Indian culture, hijras face severe harassment and discrimination from mainstream people in society, are not allowed to have any systematized source of income, and from the police that arrests them for begging, one of the few sources they have of eking out a livelihood. Nevertheless Indian society has undergone a substantial change in terms of modern and progressive outlook still people face severe threat to their lives in the name of honor killing, if they desire to be their own self. The general view held by the people is that Indian society is intolerant to the practice of homosexuality but as per view of Dattani the issue exists in the society and we cannot close our eyes and accept that it does not exist. The fact is that it is reality and has to be accepted. As Dattani avers "In any case, being gay or lesbian is not right or wrong, it is reality and we have to learn to accept alternate relationship and live with them" (Menon, 2003). However, the silence on the issue has been broken in the recent times, at large. In the last two decades homosexuality has become increasingly visible in the print and audio-visual media. Ashok Row Kavi avers about his 'coming out' experience in an interview that

> When you come out in India, gay identity becomes your primary identity. If you come out as an openly homosexual man and refuse to get married to a woman, then your homosexual identity becomes a form of rebellion and attracts a great deal of attention. All the other identities being a good journalist, for instance become back-ups. When I came out in 1984, I didn't realize it would create such a ruckus, but I nearly lost my job. (2008)

The verdict has brought the issue out of the rug, still it has to go a long way to garner consensus on the subject as it has its own pros and cons. The acceptance of homosexuality on the societal level is still a matter of debate. Decriminalization of homosexuality does not mean to extol and promote the transgressive behaviour rather to provide freedom of choice without harming others and to get adequate space to be an individual, oneself, without fear of penalization. Dattani implores for a change in our fixed perceptions and inflexible notions and become more accepting of all people notwithstanding of their sexual orientation and let them live without any fear or guilt. He clarifies his viewpoint regarding the issue that "In any case, being gay or lesbian is not right or wrong, it is reality and we have to learn to accept alternate relationships and live with them" (Rao, 2003). Through his plays, he wants to make homosexuality acceptable and to be tolerated, by sensitizing people for in the modern world only homosexuals are still stigmatized as a group, in a widespread pattern subsuming nationality, ethnic group, race, religion and social and economic class, seeking autonomy they continue to be deprived of certain freedoms, struggle to free themselves from the cultural and social oppressive outlooks.

Works Cited

Agarwal, Beena. *Mahesh Dattani's Plays: A New Horizon in Indian Theatre*. Jaipur, Book Enclave, 2008. Print.

Campaign for Lesbian Rights. "Lesbian Emergence". *Women's Studies in India: A Reader* ed. Mary E. John. New Delhi: Penguin Books, 2008. Print.

Chaudhuri, Asha Kuthari. *Mahesh Dattani*. New Delhi: Foundation Books, 2005. Print.

Dattani, Mahesh. *Collected Plays*. New Delhi: Penguin Books, 2000. Print.

——. *Collected Plays*. Vol. 2. New Delhi: Penguin Books, 2002. Print.

George, Miruna. "Constructing the Self and the Other: *Seven Steps Around the Fire* and *Bravely Fought the Queen*". *Mahesh Dattani's Plays: Critical Perspectives*. ed. Angelie Multani. New Delhi: Pencraft International, 2007. Print.

Ghosh, Sohini. "Foreword". *Gandhi's Tiger and Sita's Smile* ed. Ruth Vanita. New Delhi: Yoda Press, 2005. Print.

Kavi, Ashok Row. "An Interview with Ashok Row Kavi-Coming Out in India". N.P., March 2008. Web. 8 July 2012.

Mee, Erin B. "Invisible Issues: An Interview with Mahesh Dattani". *Mahesh Dattani's Plays: Critical Perspectives* ed. Angelie Multani. New Delhi: Pencraft International, 2007. Print.

Menon, Rajiv and K.S. Prakash. "Theatre to Morning Raga…". *hinduonnet.com. The Hindu*. Hyderabad, 2 July 2003. Web.

Rao, Kshama. "Mahesh Dattani". *bordercrossings.org. The Gentleman*, 2003. Web.

Schoene, Berthold. "Queer Politics, Queer Theory, and the Future of "Identity": Spiraling Out of Culture". *The Cambridge Companion to Feminist Literary Theory* ed. Ellen Rooney. Chennai: Cambridge University Press, 2006. Print.

Vanita, Ruth. *Gandhi's Tiger and Sita's Smile*. New Delhi: Yoda Press, 2005. Print.

Vanita, Ruth and Saleem Kidwai. *Same-Sex Love in India: Readings from Literature and History* ed. New Delhi: Macmillan India, 2001. Print.

——. "Reclaiming Gay India with Ruth Vanita". *gaytoday.com. Gay Today*: Interview, 2002. Web.

13

Problems of Accepting the 'Other' in *On a Muggy Night in Mumbai*

Shoaib Ekram

A playwright of high stature in contemporary India, famous for critiquing society, a stalwart in textualising and staging alternative sexuality and focusing his X-ray eyes on conflicts between salacious behaviour of heteronormativity and homoeroticity, Mahesh Dattani makes a daring effort, perhaps the first time in our country, to drag on a public stage what is socially deemed as taboo but yet enjoyed and becomes a living reality through his play *On a Muggy Night in Mumbai* (1998). Judith Butler, in this connection, encapsulates that sexuality is thought of in terms of heterosexual marriage that legitimates the relationship and all sexual relationships outside the purview of sanctifying law become illegal and untenable. Such conservative traditions not only enforce the distinction between legitimate and illegitimate queer lives, but also produce distinction among forms of illegitimacy and marginalised from the main stream of society and deemed as "Other". Writes Butler:

> The stable pair who would marry if only they could are cast as currently illegitimate, but eligible for a future legitimacy, whereas sexual agents who function outside the purview of marriage bond and its recognised, if illegitimate, alternative forms now constitute sexual possibilities that will never be eligible for a translation into legitimacy. (Butler, 2002: 18)

Dattani's play, *On a Muggy Night in Mumbai*, successfully visualises all such conflicts and issues. The proposition that marriage should become the only way to sanction or legitimate human sexuality is now unacceptable. Moreover, the link between, cultural norms, institution, legality, desires, and sexuality have to be debated keeping "gayness" in mind. Gay and lesbian relations are now a challenge to the nuclear family unit. Homoeroticity is emerging with a variant such as gays desire to bring up children, lesbians hatred for bearing children, and debunking monogamy to counter the established, the ideal notion of a heterosexual family. Dattani's plays concretize many subsequent writers, especially figures like Hanif Kureishi, Shyam Selvadurai, Leela Gandhi who also talk about the race-sexual identity axis.

The play was first performed at the Tata Theatre, Mumbai on 23rd of November, 1998 and was later adopted by Sanjeev Shah as a screenplay. The play deals with the emotions of those who are excluded from the mainstream of society. The play comprises of complex and conflictual situations. Every act is a potential text. The dramatic technique of Dattani brings out the true potential and nature of the characters present in the play.

The play challenges the preconceived notion of 'love' and 'marriage' which is prevalent in the society. Dattani takes the notion of love to an almost different level where it transcends the boundary of sex. The sexual urges arising in an individual find fulfilment in the opposite sex, and not with someone belonging to the same sex because that would go against the social norms. Dattani through his work speaks for that section of society which still needs to be spoken for. He foregrounds such individuals and makes them speak before the public with courage.

The play deals with emotions of love and betrayals that do exist in any relationship but the only difference is that the relationship which is being talked about here does not have the sanction of society. The unflinching and unconditional love that Kamlesh harbours for Prakash is no less weak than the intensity seen in a heterosexual relationship. Despite knowing the fact that Prakash is no longer in love with him and decides to lead a heterosexual life, Kamlesh keeps quiet. Prakash even changes his name to Ed. No one, except Kamlesh knows that Ed and Prakash are one and the same. And when Prakash reveals his full name as Edwin Prakash Mathew everyone is furious at him. They even decide to tell Kiran the truth about him but Kamlesh stops them;

> Sharad: Are you mad? You must be mad!
>
> Deepali: You must tell her!
>
> Kamlesh: You promised! All of you! It doesn't exist.
>
> Sharad: You tricked us! You tricked us to it!
>
> Kamlesh: No.
>
> (Dattani, 2000, Act I, 79)

He does not want to expose the truth of Prakash to his sister Kiran whom he proposes to marry. He also does so because of the sufferings which her sister had to undergo due to the bad experience of her past marriage. Kamlesh suffers in silence.

The play as we know deals with the same sex relationship which our society forbids. And in such a society it is nearly impossible for such a relationship to bloom. Thus, there are only two choices left before them; either they hide themselves under the garb of 'normal' people or they flee from the country for the west. Prakash takes the former route whereas Bunny and Ranjit take recluse in the latter. The former's choice is even more difficult to live with because in such a situation the individuals dangle between two identities; one to which the individual docs not belong and the other from which the individual is running away.

Ranjit who leaves the country for the west is happier as compared to his friends back home. He leads his life the way he wants without negotiations, compromises and fearing the society. He says, "Ranjit: Call me what you will. My English lover and I have been together for twelve years now. You lot will never be able to find a lover in this wretched country!" (Dattani, 2000, Act I, 71).

Even Bunny advises Kamlesh to get married to a girl and continue his feeling as a gay. Bunny himself is married and well set. This is his way of having what is denied to him. He advises Kamlesh to follow the norms of the society and at the same time have his way to fulfil his own sexual desire as Dattani has presented in his another play *Do the Needful* where Alpesh Patel, a gay and Lata Gouda, sick for her sexual fantasies with a terrorist Salim. Bunny convinces him as, "Bunny: Since you want us to help you let me give you some advice. You are looking in the wrong places to forget your Prakash. Get married" (Dattani, 2000, Act I, 70).

Bunny fails to understand the turmoil inside Kamlesh's mind. Kamlesh suffers in silence for he cannot reveal his pain to anyone because that would jeopardize the marriage of his sister. He also undergoes psychiatrist treatment but that also proves of little help. His suffering is way deeper than that which can be cured. He says:

> Kamlesh: I knew I needed medication. I chose the psychiatrist out of the yellow pages. He pretended to understand. Until he began to tell me about aversion therapy. For a while, I believed him. Because the medication helped me cope with my depression better. Until he said I would never be happy as a gay man. It is impossible to change society, he said, but it may be possible for you to reorient yourself. (Dattani, 2000, Act I, 69)

Kamlesh finds it nearly impossible to separate himself from Prakash's thoughts within him. The entire play revolves around his inability to free himself from Prakash. All the characters present take turns to suggest their views regarding freeing Kamlesh from depression. Sharad advises Kamlesh to destroy the last photograph of Prakash with him. Kamlesh hesitates to do it and at his juncture Kiran enters. Kiran is eager to introduce her fiancé to his brother. Kamlesh is filled with sorrow but can't express it. He, in fact, puts on a happy face for the sake of his sister. Dattani artistically manages to portray such a conflictual situation in a rather beautiful way. There is tension and conflict inside Kamlesh's mind. He is torn apart between his sister's happiness and his sexual urges. He sacrifices his own feelings for her sister's sake.

Deepali is a character who is bold and confident. She is frank and content with her lesbian relationship. She decides to tell Kiran the truth about Prakash by showing her the photograph of Kamlesh and Prakash in which they are "Cheek to cheek, pelvis to pelvis. Naked" (Dattani, 2000, Act I, 71-72). And when Bunny objects to this idea, she says, "Deepali: She must know the truth! She thinks she is marrying someone who loves her very much" (Dattani, 2000, Act II, 84).

Sharad also supports her. It seems surprising how the society looks at a gay/lesbian relationship. It equates it with something which is wrong, something which is evil. Even the characters present in the play are compelled to acknowledge this:

> Kamlesh: He goes to church every week now. They put him on to a psychiatrist. He believes his love for me was the work of the devil. Now the devil has left him.
>
> Sharad: Now the devil has put him on to your sister. I'll tell you what. Show her the photograph. Let her know who the devil is.
>
> (Dattani, 2000, Act II, 85)

The dramatist very beautifully portrays the dilemma of Kamlesh. He is torn apart between his feelings. He is ready to accept that his love for Prakash was the work of devil. The dramatist brings out the plight of such people who are constantly pushed into oblivion by the cruel society. The only solace, Kamlesh finds, is in the photograph, the only souvenir which he clings on to.

The third act begins with the lusty cries of the *baraat,* the marriage party. The loud noise and the pomp show do not seem interesting to the characters present in the living room of Kamlesh. The world of homosexuals is dark, hidden due to the fear of society. Ranjit shuts the window to faint the loud sound of the *baraat*. The opening and shutting of the window is symbolic. Shutting of the window here represents shutting of the world outside. The world of the homosexuals is still confined within the four walls of a room. It represents the small space which they carve for themselves. The world of heterosexual is that of light whereas the homosexuals are constantly in dark. Prakash who now pretends to be heterosexual does not feel the same; he opens the window and says:

> **Ed:** Look around you. Look outside. (Goes to the window and flingsit open.) Look at that wedding crowd! There are real men and women out there! You have to see them to know what I mean. But you don't want to. You don't want to look at the world outside this...this den of yours. All of you want to live in your own little bubble. (Dattani, 2000, Act III, 99)

The dramatist through his play aptly puts forth the issues of marriage—both conventional and unconventional. The dramatist shows a failed and troubled conventional marriage in Kiran, in Bunny the dramatist shows us how a homosexual through a garb of conventional marriage continues his love for the same sex. The very institution of marriage has been satirized.

Dattani presents the dilemma of the Indian homosexuals who have two different mindsets. The one that realizes the importance of heterosexual man and the power they exercise, they consider them as 'real' man-woman. The other mindset is represented by the people who are content with their present identity as a 'pure gay'. Prakash represents the former mindset whereas Deepali represents the latter.

Dattani takes a dig at the society that does not give any scope for the gays to fulfil their desires. The constant fear of being marginalized by the society makes them look for other alternatives. They know that if they fulfil their longings of being gay they would be damaging their reputation and identity. Their sexuality is suppressed and killed by the rules and regulations of the society. Dattani challenges the conservative Indian society with its hypocrisies. His characters are at constant conflict with the society, longing of its approval.

What is very fascinating about the play is bold and frank treatment to gay theme given by the dramatist. Depiction of gay theme calls for guts and courage on the part of the dramatist. Dattani handles this postmodernistic issue in a very daring way.

He puts the whole issue in a very dynamic way. He has instilled courage and the spirit into the minds of his characters that they can openly reveal their gay identity that is evidenced through Kamlesh's remark, "Let them talk! If two men want to love one another, what's the harm?" (Dattani, 2000, Act II, 91).

Works Cited

Agrawal, Beena. *Mahesh Dattani's Plays: A New Horizon in Indian Theatre*. Jaipur, India: Book Enclave, 2008. Print.

Butler, Judith. *Gender Trouble: Feminism and the Subversion of Identity.* London and New York: Routledge, 1990. 2002: 18. Print.

——. "Is Kinship Always Heterosexual?", *Differences*. 13 (1): 14-44. Print.

——. *Bodies That Matter*. London and New York: Routledge, 1993: 228-29. Print.

Chakrabarti, Santosh. "Gray Areas: Dattani's World of Drama" in *The Dramatic World of Mahesh Dattani: A Critical Exploration*, edited by Amarnath Prasad, New Delhi: Sarup Book Publication Pvt. Ltd., 2009. Print.

Chaudhuri, Asha Kuthari. *Contemporary Indian Writers in English Mahesh Dattani*, New Delhi: Foundation Books Pvt. Ltd., Cambridge House, 2005. Print.

Das, Bijay Kumar. *Form and Meaning in Mahesh Dattani's Plays*, New Delhi: Atlantic Publishers & Distributors (P) Ltd., 2008. Print.

Dattani, Mahesh. "Do the Needful". *Collected Plays: Critical Perspectives*. New Delhi: Penguin Books, 2000. Print.

——. *Collected Plays: Mahesh Dattani,* New Delhi: Penguin Books, 2000. Print.

McRae, John. *"A note on the play". On a Muggy Night in Mumbai, in Collected Plays Mahesh Dattani,* New Delhi: Penguin Books, 2000. Print.

Nayar, Pramod K. *Postcolonial Literature: An Introduction*. New Delhi: Pearson, 2011. Print.

Uniyal, Ranu. "Conversing with Mahesh Dattani" in *The Plays of Mahesh Dattani: A Critical Response*. (Ed.) R.K. Dhawan and Tanu Pant, New Delhi: Prestige Books, 2005. Print.

14

Dattani's *The Big Fat City*: A Modern Waste Land

Ashish Kumar Sharma

> The audience have to finish in their own heads what the playwright began.[1]
>
> —Dattani

An experimentalist into human psychology and observer of social and cultural dynamism, Mahesh Dattani undertakes a life-long project for understanding the cause/s of fascination for economic ambiance, turbulence in human behaviour, complicated lifestyles and wizard realities of human existence and collapse of humanist social order equipped with coordination, cooperation and tolerance. His play *The Big Fat City* (2014) examines boom of corporate culture, its ideology, materialism and mechanism that has resulted in decadence, degradation, (de)establishment, deconstruction of human essence which Rousseau, Wordsworth, Emerson, Gandhi, Tagore and Sri Aurobindo ever talked of. The effect has, consequently, given birth to an unreal society residing in an 'unreal city' which the modern and postmodern contemporary man calls a 'metropolitan lifestyle'—a life of "I" rather than of "we", totally irresponsive, irrational and inhuman of a haphazard mentality.

In the play *The Big Fat City* of Dattani the word "fat" is a loaded term. It may denote many things such as Dattani himself, in an interview to Tutun Mukherjee, tells:

> I think the name sort of sums it up—you can look at fat as obese or fat as enormous or large or grand. The city resonates differently to different people—some people see it as exciting and glamorous, some see it as ugly in some ways. (*The Telegraph*, June 8, 2014)

Being a member of Dattani's audience I take the privilege to finish the play in my head. I found this play resounding the undertones and overtones of 'modern waste land' as he himself admits, "*The Big Fat City* is not a family drama in the mould that I am used to writing. It is a breakaway play for me. It is, in fact, three stories set in the city that merge on one eventful night" (*The Telegraph*, June 8, 2014).

The 'resonance' in the perception of the city leads Mumbai in Dattani's play *The Big Fat City*, in Eliot's terms, is a prototype of the unreal city. The city of Mumbai in Indian context, a 'Maya Nagri' (The city of illusion/s) is, in correlative term, the London of India which deserves to be called a replica of 'modern waste land' for Eliot's has become now an 'old Waste Land'. Dattani's modern waste land is a re-emergence of what existed in England hence ninety-two years back, approximately a century. This evidences that the changing conditions of human mind that began in the first world countries in the beginning of 20th century has claimed its reoccurrence in the Third World countries like India, Pakistan, and Sri Lanka, Bhutan, etc. Thus, Dattani's Mumbai stands as the representative of metropolitan cities of the Third World.

The objective of comparing Dattani's *The Big Fat City* with that of Eliot's *The Waste Land* is not to draw parallels on the basis of formal and genre properties but to link the essence of both the works through central themes which is an effect of over professionalism and mechanical life in a metropolitan city. The set of three stories merging with an eventful night are just like Eliot's five sections rather five different poems merged to make one whole poem. Preparations for show-off in a 'shooting scene' made by the characters Lalita Jagtiani, Kailash, Sailesh, Rahul, Anu, Puneet, Harjeet, Murali and Niharika draws parallels with the first section of *The Waste Land*, 'The Burial of the Dead'.

These characters are spiritually dead for they, while plotting the 'play within play' in *The Big Fat City* just to take money, befooling others, having no human sentiments for one another. Anu tricks her own caring brother Harjeet. Almost everyone is playing the game against one another that can be linked to the second section of the poem, "A Game of Chess". In their games they do not care even life of their close ones also.

After the death of her husband, Lolly embraces a runaway marriage with Sailesh instead of feeling any shock or even grief for the loss of her life partner. It seems that she was waiting for his death so that she could liberate herself for her sex fantasies. The change in Lolly's behaviour is an evidence of the death of the sanctity of marriage and faith in bond between conjugal loves. It indicates that the sentiments of marital relationship were burnt in the fire of her lust, the physical thirst which draws parallels with the Eliot's third section 'The Fire Sermon'. Lolly's urgent need for uniting with Sailesh claims the death of love and of faith as well. The desire for physical satiety and personal pleasures has killed the other aspects of life such that humanity, faith and love. In a metropolitan city, rich class takes alcohol for energy to revitalize and make themselves ready for bed after official exhaustion all day long but in Dattani's play, for Lolly's husband Kailash it is an addiction that causes his death, however, because of its overdose. Here, death of the drunkard, 'the death by alcohol', makes affinity with the Eliot's the fourth section 'Death by Water'.

Coherence of Dattani's Mumbai in *The Big Fat City* with that of the Eliot's London in *The Waste Land* underlines that "the waste land is a recurring phenomenon." Dattani is the name in the history of Indian English Drama that has dominated not only the local and national stage but also the postmodern contemporary international stage. His plays, *Tara* (1990), *A Brief Candle*, *Where There is a Will* (1988), *Final Solutions* (1993), *Where Did I Leave My Purdah*? (2014), etc. deal with a variety of themes and issues. A man of multiple aspects, creativity and identities, Dattani, through his plays, has played a prominent role in shaping and modernizing Indian theatre with scientific objectivity. He is contemporary in terms of choosing not only vibrant language and innovative theatrical techniques but also in capturing the contemporary realities. His plays have naturalistic and surrealistic representation of human life and thematically cross the linguistic and cultural boundaries. By applying naturalistic approach he lays bare the hypocrisies, politics and entrenched belief of the society, dramatizes the stereotypical representations of the individuals and unravels the multiple prototypical masks imposed on them. Dattani's recent play *The Big Fat City*, to a great extent, thematically resembles to Eliot's theme of *The Waste Land* being an 'immense panorama of futility and anarchy'. The city of Mumbai which is the representative of metropolitan cities corresponds to the Eliot's notion of 'the unreal city' in *The Waste Land*.

Dattani's *The Big Fat City,* set in an apartment of Mumbai is a black comedy that brings to the fore the gruesome realities of the metropolitan culture. It unmasks the reality of the false faces and pretentions of ordinary people in metros where they are entangled between extraordinary situations. Although, superficially, the play is comic in performance yet at deeper levels portrays the miseries of postmodern bits of luxuries. The play has multiple stories fused together—a corporate couple Murali and Niharika are caught in a perplexed situation because of bearing the false mask of affluence, a very feature of contemporary mechanical life that throws them in financial crisis; a famous TV star Lalita Jagtiani alias Lolly in her late forties is facing a tough time of her career and has troubled marriage; a young aspiring actress Anu has shocking secrets of her familial and love life with puneet.

The play begins with a scene in a multi-story apartment—an emblem of metropolitan culture of Mumbai and like cities where a couple Murali (who has lost his job) and Niharika invite Murali's old friend Sailesh for dinner with a plan to get some financial support from him so that they could clear off their home loan. In spite of their pathetic condition, they prefer to falsely show off a higher standard and confidence. While they are in conversation, Lolly, resident of the adjacent flat of the same apartment enters in a pre-planned way with bottles of wine in her hands leaving her 'merry-making' son Rahul and her drunkard husband Kailash in her flat. Her son, the so-called founder of

Anti-tobacco club and a green peace activist, is a confidant of his mother's secrets. Later on we come to know that he was arrested in a drug case. Kailash who is Lolly's drunkard husband is a man who is unintentionally murdered by Puneet in Murali's flat. Niharika's so-called younger sister, Anu, has come to Mumbai assuming herself an aspiring actress and has a secret plan of marrying her boyfriend Puneet who unintentionally, becomes the accomplice of Kailash's murder because of confusion. After Kailash's coincidental murder, the characters are unmasked and their real selves come to us. Lolly is trapped in a pathetic situation because of her son Rahul's arrest for smuggling and meets a worst situation. Murali and Niharika along with others try to bring out Lolly's son Rahul from the police custody that has been arrested in a drug smuggling case. Meanwhile, Harjeet, Anu's brother from Haryana becomes aware of their secret plan and shoots Anu and her boyfriend Puneet in a dramatic way. Harjeet's behaviour is a representative of the orthodox mindset and the honor-killing culture prevalent in his native region Haryana. All this bru-ha-ha becomes the news for television channels and "The Mumbai Mirror" magazine. Finally, Lolly moves with Sailesh selling her flat to Usmaan Bhai and settles in Karjat. Usman presents 'a painting of city of Mumbai' to Niharika and Murali which shows the crowd and fast pace life of the metro cities. Murali and Niharika moves to Thirunaalvelli which is Murali's place with a promise to come back to meet in Mumbai again.

Mumbai in Dattani's play marks the death of human emotions, sentiments, love, relationships and values yet people keep busy themselves in one or other activities as if preparing to burry all these dead underneath. The death of sentiments reminds us of Eliots "The Burial of the Dead". In the play, we see the death of faith in the relationships between Anu and Puneet. The warmth that is the essence of any relationship has been buried and it has turned mechanical. The episode where Anu assumes herself an actress and talks to her boyfriend Puneet who in turn doubts on her affair with the actor, indicates towards the death of faith between them.

> ANU: (on the phone). No Darling, You are not listening. Sweetheart, just li....
>
> But he never... (Inside the bedroom more aggressive) Just shut up! Shut your face! Fuck you! He just put his arm around me and kissed me on the cheeks. All think I am having an affair with him, so be it! Yes I am sleeping around with that dodo. That's why I am struggling along, right? Ya, I'am sleeping with him. He is right here in my bedroom. (Dattani, 2014: 169)

Another evidence of Puneet's suspicion on Anu is observed when he starts spying to find her love affair with someone else. This spying episode has wider implications on the ultramodern industrial society. Dattani, through this play perhaps, wants to say that the mechanical relationship and craving for material gains always result in the shift of priorities in the life and that ultimately makes the relationship 'unreal' and weakens the bond and makes it fragile to be broken at any time. Lolly, famous TV star in the play has unreliable marriage. Her husband Kailash is a drunkard and not the bond between conjugal love but wine is his first passion. Consequently, Lolly develops a soft corner for Sailesh unhesitatingly and she finally unites with him to be one just after the death of her husband. By this quick run-way marriage, it becomes clear that for her, her husband's sudden death is not a matter of grief rather a brilliant opportunity to be cashed off and get rid of him. Her indifference towards Kailash can well be evidenced with her following exchange of messages in their mobiles:

> SCREEN (from Niharika): KAILASH IS HERE. COME WITH BANWARI AND CARRY HIM HOME. They take Kailash to the bedroom. Niharika gets a message.
>
> SCREEN (from Lolly): OH NO, NOT AGAIN! NIKKI DUMP HIM IN A CORNER SOMEWHERE PLEASE. RAHUL'S PARTY IS IN FULL SWING. I AM SORTING SOME THINGS OUT.
>
> (Dattani, 2014: 175)

The residents of the unreal city are always fascinated towards luxury, show off rather are trapped within the circumference of pomp and show, therefore, get no time or they have no feel for the essence of real life residing in real city. They apply their intelligence in dark practices and playing big games instead of thinking of perfection of their life giving artistic finish to mark an impression of beauty in life. Instead of struggling for cooperation, human concern and instead of exploring the gist of life and values of relationship, they ignore the truth of life and keep themselves busy in befooling their close ones—relatives, family members and friends for their very material gains. In the play, we see that almost every character hatches one or the other secret plot working simultaneously in their minds. They pass their lives on razor's edge. To escape their downfall or collapse they play various dirty games against one another. There are games within game in the form of plans/plots whether it is crisis management of Murali and Niharika by befooling Sailesh or Anu's secret plan for marrying her boyfriend and of fanciful career as an actress or Lolly's secret smuggling of drugs. All these games are symbolic representations of the disbelief that has occurred in family relations, blood relations and more disappointedly human relations.

If Eliot's *The Waste Land* represents the death of religion, emotions and sentiments from human life in contemporary England and more particularly the city of London, Dattani's *The Big Fat City* portrays the multiple deaths due to the fascination for luxury life, getting maximum wealth in zero effort and the growing professionalism. People are running after the money and are, therefore, ready to go to any extent for that as is proved by Lolly's involvement in drugs smuggling for monetary gains without caring for her fame as a TV star. Relationships and emotions have gone to secondary place. The characters in the play falsely propagate about their wealth and positions even in their situation of acute financial crisis. All this consequently results in their spiritual emptiness and converts them into machines.

Note

1. Mahesh Dattani in an interview with Tutun Mukherjee. Culcutta: *The Telegraph*. June 8. 2014.

Works Cited

Agrawal, Beena. *Mahesh Dattani's Plays: A New Horizon in Indian Theatre*. Jaipur: Book Enclave, 2008. Print.

Chakrabarti, Santosh. "Gray Areas: Dattani's World of Drama" in *The Dramatic World of Mahesh Dattani: A Critical Exploration*. ed. Amarnath Prasad. New Delhi: Sarup Book Publication Pvt. Ltd., 2009. Print.

Chaudhuri, Asha Kuthari. *Contemporary Indian Writers in English Mahesh Dattani*. New Delhi: Foundation Books Pvt. Ltd., Cambridge House, 2005: 57. Print.

Das, Bijay Kumar. *Form and Meaning in Mahesh Dattani's Plays*. New Delhi: Atlantic Publishers & Distributors (P) Ltd., 2008. Print.

Dattani, Mahesh. Preface, *Collected Plays: Mahesh Dattani*. New Delhi: Penguin Books, 2000. Print.

Eliot, T.S. "The Waste Land." *Anthology of Modern American Poetry*. Ed. Cary Nelson. NY: Oxford University Press, 2000. Print.

Hutcheon, Linda. *A Poetics of Postmodernism: History, Theory, Fiction*. London and New York: Routledge, 1988. Print.

Walsmley, Chris Snipp. "Postmodernism" in *Literary Theory and Criticism*. Ed. Patricia Waugh. New Delhi: Oxford University Press, 2012. Print.

Waugh, Patricia. *Literary Theory and Criticism*. India: Oxford University Press, 2012. Print.